SIMPLY MINDFUL

A 7-WEEK COURSE AND PERSONAL HANDBOOK FOR MINDFUL LIVING

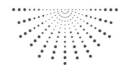

DONALD ALTMAN

SIMPLY MINDFUL

Published by: Moon Lake Media

info@mindfulpractices.com

Cover Design: BGHanson Graphic Design

Illustrations by Paul Mendoza

ISBN: 9780963916174

Publisher's Cataloging-in-Publication Data

Names: Altman, Donald

Title: Simply mindful: a 7-week course and personal handbook for mindful living / Donald Altman.

Identifiers: ISBN 9780963916174 (pbk.)

Description: Portland, OR : Moon Lake Media, 2020. | Includes bibliographical references. | Summary: Presents a structured 7-week course on mindfulness, including a historical overview of traditional mindfulness and its role in Buddhism, and how mindfulness is used in Western healthcare. Explains the concept of mindfulness, along with 36 integrated skills, or practices, for stress, relationships, creativity, and productivity.

Subjects: LCSH: Buddhism -- Doctrines. | Mindfulness-based cognitive therapy -- Handbooks, manuals, etc. | Mind and body. | BISAC: SELF-HELP / Personal Growth / General. | SELF-HELP / Self-Management / Stress Management. | SELF-HELP / Creativity.

Classification: LCC BF637.M56 A48 2020 | DDC 158.12 A48S56--dc23

ABOUT THE AUTHOR

Donald Altman, MA, LPC, is a psychotherapist, award-winning author, and former Buddhist monk. Featured in The Mindfulness Movie and profiled in the Living Spiritual Teachers Project, he has written over 15 books that teach how to incorporate mindfulness into daily life.

Award-winning books include:

The Mindfulness Toolbox—winner of two Gold IBPA Benjamin Franklin™ Awards as best book in the "Psychology" and "Body-Mind-Spirit" categories, Clearing Emotional Clutter —selected "One of the Best Spiritual Books of 2016" and The Mindfulness Code—chosen "One of the Best Spiritual Books of 2010."

Donald served his community as vice-president of The Center for Mindful Eating and as an adjunct professor in Portland State University's Interpersonal Neurology Certificate Program and at Lewis and Clark Graduate School of Education and Counseling. He travels internationally, spreading seeds of mindfulness as a health and business consultant, keynote speaker, and mindfulness workshop leader. He lives in Portland, Oregon, enjoying the beauty and awe of nature with his beloved wife, family and friends.

mindfulpractices.com

facebook.com/mndfulpractices

Travelers all, on this blue planet—

May we find our true purpose
by helping those travelers
we encounter each day,
in ways both large and small.

And, as an ancient blessing advises—

May suffering ones be suffering free,
May the fear struck fearless be,
May grieving ones shed all grief,
May all beings find relief.

And as we awaken,
May we all travel in peace.

ACKNOWLEDGMENTS

It is only with the help of many teachers, students, persons and spiritual friends that this book is possible. For all those who I have met in workshops or online, thank you for sharing your spirit, life experiences and inspiration.

I will always be thankful for the compassionate teachings of the Venerable U. Silananda, and his example as a teacher. My spiritual brother and devoted Buddhist scholar, U. Thitzana. Randy Fitzgerald, a friend through the years, for his support, creative spark and wise feedback. My cousin John Babbitt, who has infused this project with his levity, creativity, and above all, his caring nature. Bruce Hanson, a friend and artist whose design flair enhanced all that is in these pages.

I am grateful and indebted to my family, especially my mother Barbara, a shining light and spiritual guide in my life. Finally, my Bak'u del cuore Maria, my soul friend and life partner, for recognizing and dancing with the possible and beautiful.

BOOKS BY DONALD ALTMAN

Reflect: Awaken to the Wisdom of the Here and Now

The Mindfulness Toolbox

Clearing Emotional Clutter

One Minute Mindfulness

101 Mindful Ways to Build Resilience

The Mindfulness Code

Living Kindness

The Mindfulness Toolbox for Relationships

Art of the Inner Meal

Meal by Meal

Stay Mindful & Color

The Joy Compass

Eat, Savor, Satisfy: 12-Weeks to Mindful Eating

.

CONTENTS

INTRODUCTION

Imagine turning on the news and hearing the following story: "Scientists today announced the discovery of a new, all-natural vitamin that reduces stress and high blood pressure with no side effects." The story goes on to state that this vitamin can be taken by anyone at any age because it contains no harmful substances and has no side effects—except for feeling more tranquil, mentally focused, resilient, compassionate, patient, and joyful. You're expecting to hear something disparaging, like it must cost a million bucks! Just then the news anchor concludes the story by saying, "And by the way, did I mention the cost? It's absolutely free!"

Would you take the vitamin?

That vitamin as you've guessed is what *Simply Mindful* offers in these pages. Whether you are someone wanting to know more about mindfulness merely for your own use, or whether you are curious about how mindfulness could benefit you and others in a workplace setting, this book was designed with you in mind. It's called *Simply Mindful* because you don't need any previous background to use the practices and material here. And yet, my purpose in writing this book was for it to go beyond being just another "how-to learn mindfulness" book. Here's what I mean:

> ***Simply Mindful* is a practical handbook for improving the quality of your life through specific life-affirming skills designed to increase your overall well-being, at home, work, school and other environments.**

In this sense, mindfulness can be understood as a medicine, or antidote for the increased demands of modern life—which can easily throw anyone off balance. These pages will clearly illustrate that mindfulness is a practice and a skill that anyone can learn in order to find the joy in life, as well as reduce suffering from life's challenges.

Most fundamentally, mindfulness is the means by which you can change your *relationship* to those difficult aspects of your life. This is why I like to refer to mindfulness as *an inside job*. Mindfulness supports a more spacious awareness, so that we're less prone to reactivity and negativity.

Spoiler Alert: *This won't stop rude drivers from cutting you off or turn an insensitive boss into a caring leader.*

With mindfulness, we develop the mental habit of viewing persons and events—even those annoying and difficult ones—with a more curious, compassionate and welcoming perspective. To demonstrate, let's try a brief mental experiment.

Right now, think of an annoying event that occurred recently. Maybe someone cut you off while you were driving. Maybe you couldn't meet a deadline for a work, school or other project. Maybe you were stuck behind a long line people at the store. Whatever your annoyance, what were you feeling in that moment?

Now let's imagine we could turn back the clock. Only this time, you'll re-experience the event as if you possessed a newfound superpower—the ability *to be like teflon* to whatever comes your way. Actually, your superpower is the ability to be more open, curious, accepting, grateful and compassionate. For example, if your annoyance was with another person, your superpower would open your tender heart—so you would be aware of how that person might have been late for an appointment or not feeling well. You could also use your superpower to shift your attention to be more curious toward something you could have gratitude for—even during that annoying event.

Again, visualize a do-over of that annoying event, only this time picture yourself using your teflon superpower of compassion, curiosity and gratitude. What does this feel like?

I hope that gives you a taste of what's possible with mindfulness. As you gain these skills, you'll be more able to experience the freedom that comes from not reacting to negativity or attaching yourself to those things that produce suffering. As your suffering reduces, you'll start to notice the joy that is possible and present in your life.

To use a weather metaphor, mindfulness helps you locate calm during the stormiest and most stressful of conditions. Think of *Simply Mindful* as a kindly guide who is ready to share skills and useful information with you—so you can participate in your life in a meaningful and purposeful way.

AN EASY-TO-FOLLOW, LIFE AFFIRMING ROADMAP

The roadmap for *Simply Mindful* is straightforward, consisting of three key elements: concepts, research and skills. The concepts and research studies will give you new insights, as well as help you understand how selective attention is a powerful engine for rewiring the brain. However, if research is not your cup of tea, you can always skip ahead to the skills and exercises.

Simply Mindful is filled with experiential practices that you can apply daily. I like to think of these practices as seeds that will take root in your own "mindful garden of the mind and body." These can easily be adapted for various situations, and they are at the core how you will gain mindfulness skills that will take root, grow and flourish over time. I recommend practicing these experiences starting from the beginning because each skill prepares you for the next one.

Chapter 1, *Well-Being Is Your Birthright* investigates the original meaning of mindfulness, which I hope delights and surprises you. This chapter will explore several neuroscience "brain myths" as it invites you into the shallow end of the mindfulness pool with new here and now awareness experiences.

Chapter 2, *Secrets of the Organic Here and Now*, explores the nature of mind and how often we are *missing in action* when it comes to being in the present moment. You'll discover how to engage the breath in order to contact deep awareness that can transform your mind and your life.

Chapter 3, *All-Natural Ingredients for Daily Mindfulness*, includes the development of positive daily habits without which mindfulness would be severely hindered or impossible. Accessing mindfulness requires a number of activities for supporting the brain and body, including proper sleep, nutrition that supports mental clarity, boundary setting with technology, tuning up through movement, and other refreshing behaviors.

Chapter 4, *Enhance Working Environments with Wellness*, acknowledges that we sometimes encounter unwelcome or toxic environments. Whether through a culture of overwork, a negative environment, unclear expectations from a manager or teacher, or a co-worker's behavior, it is essential that we cultivate self-care, in addition to finding healthy ways of coping and relating to others.

Chapter 5, *Invite Mindfulness into Heart and Home*, extends the invitation of deep peace into your abode. Here, you'll explore ideas for creating a sacred space where you can find silence and peace, which is vital to your physical, spiritual and mental health. You will also explore an ancient practice designed to enlarge compassion as it helps overcome fear, mistrust and other negative emotions.

Chapter 6, *Reflection and the Power of Pause*, describes a four-part *reflect* practice for pausing from the hectic and chaotic times of your day. As you'll discover, the practice of reflecting and looking inward utilizes and strengthens what is the most integrative and human part of the brain. Gratitude plays an important role here, too, as it aligns us to our world in a thoughtful way that emphasizes hope, resilience and joy.

Chapter 7, *Re-mindfulness for Staying Balanced*, ties together all that you have accomplished in this book, and offers a six-step method for maintaining and growing your mindfulness skills.

An *Index of Experiences and Exercises* follows the last chapter. Here is where you will find a chapter-by-chapter list of all 36 experiences in *Simply Mindful*. In this way, you can easily locate those skills that you want to try again. I also recommend using this list as a way to craft your own, personalized mindfulness program.

Finally, if at some point you wish to seek additional resources to further deepen and enrich your practice, there's a *For Further Reading* section with lots of useful and varied materials.

Personally, I like to think that the journey into mindfulness continues anew each day. Indeed, mindfulness invites us to experience even the seemingly ordinary as something fresh, unexpected and novel. May you, too, find much delight in the unexpected as you start this journey to wholeness, healing and wellness.

WELL-BEING IS YOUR BIRTHRIGHT

*Y*ou've very likely heard the French term *déjà vu,* which is the feeling of "having been there before." That feeling of having been there before is woven into our lives. Once we experience something or someone for the first time, the novelty is gone. So, even that beautifully scented, crimson red flower that once entranced us as children becomes "just another boring rose" as we get older. As many a blues singer has sung, "The thrill is gone!"

I've often described mindfulness as being the opposite of *déjà vu.* As it so happens, the French have a term to describe that as well, and it's called *jamais vu,* or "the experience of *never* having been there before." To me, that's the childlike awareness we all once had, when even the simplest of things possessed a sense of glee and wonder. Wouldn't it be marvelous to reclaim that ability?

Interestingly, the original meaning of the word mindfulness —from the *Sanskrit* word *sati*—is "self-remembrance" and "self-recollection." In other words, mindfulness helps us regain the parts of ourselves that have been lost or fragmented because of dis-traction, dis-connection and forgetfulness. The process of self-remembering and self-recollecting brings these lost parts back home to mind-body-spirt so we can feel whole again. This is, after all, healing in its truest sense. It is no surprise that Albert Einstein wrote, "Never lose a holy curiosity." How marvelous!

ALL-NATURAL BIRTHRIGHT

While in the monastery, I had the opportunity to sit and talk with the Venerable U. Silananda, a well-known mindfulness teacher from Burma. One time he said to me, "Mindfulness is free. We are born with it." I've since thought about what he meant, and have come to understand that mindfulness is a human birthright. It is an innate capacity that exists within each of us. At the same time, it is also a skill that requires discipline and effort.

What skills have you developed in your life? Surely, you didn't pass your driver's license exam by chance or by *not* paying attention. As with any other innate capacity, whether musical or athletic, the effective use of mindfulness requires discipline and a commitment to develop greater skill over time. Once mastered, it becomes part of the flow of all that you do, bringing with it a feeling of ease and joy. Here are a couple of my favorite quotes that make this point:

Freedom is not the path to freedom.
Discipline is the path to freedom.
—Sufi master Inayat Khan, from *The Gayan*

Skillful farmers do better than random farmers.
—Lama Surya Das

What's more, anyone can understand and experience mindfulness, and you certainly don't need to meditate in the forest to attain this knowledge. You don't need to be a specialist of any kind either. As your natural birthright, mindfulness is meant to be integrated into everyday living.

Mindfulness is experiential and reflective by nature. That's because it's about cultivating a particular way of being that asks us to pay attention, be curious, and to be intentional in our lives. Furthermore, it brings the precious nature of life into focus. It helps us understand that each moment is both joyful and fragile, and therefore the most important time of our life. That mindfulness is being applied to various forms of therapy is just a measure of how effective it is at fostering balance and well-being.

A Very (Very) Brief History of Mindfulness

Understanding history has value because it lets us see where we've been and where we're headed. With that in mind, let's put mindfulness in a historical context. First, it's worth noting that practices for attaining presence and being intentional are found in all of our wisdom traditions. The ancient Christian prayer practices of Hesychasm, centering prayer and *lectio divina* (divine reading), are wonderful examples of this.

Mindfulness as a training tool played a central role in Buddhism. In fact, mindfulness has been known as the seventh element of the Noble Eightfold Path to liberation and enlightenment. Material from the historical Buddha's *suttas*, or teachings, has been collected to form what are traditionally known as the four foundations of mindfulness. Buddha often would ask adherents to meditate deeply on 1) mindfulness of the body, 2) feelings (sensations as experienced in the mind), 3) the conscious mind, and 4) the arising and falling away of phenomena, or impermanence.

Mindfulness meditation was taught by the Buddha as a type of analysis that facilitated the development of wisdom and enabled one to release attachment to reflexive thoughts and negative patterns that sabotage happiness. It's not surprising that a training for peace of mind would emerge during the late 20th century into mainstream Western mental health care.

Professor Ellen Langer and her colleagues at Harvard University did some of the early mindfulness research by focusing on aging and how mindfulness training can give elderly persons more control over their lives. The training programs enhanced both stress reduction and the overall health of participants.[1]

The following variations on mindfulness show how adaptable it is as an approach for promoting wellness. Long before its current popularity, mindfulness has been used in both pain and mental health clinics.

- *Mindfulness-Based Stress Reduction* (MBSR) is a therapeutic approach created in 1979 by Jon Kabat-Zinn and colleagues at the University of Massachusetts Medical Center. Patients with anxiety disorders or pain who attended the 8-week group program reported significant improvements in their conditions. Mindfulness techniques used in the program included sitting meditation, walking meditation, the 'body scan,' and yoga. (The body scan is a guided sensory awareness exercise that will be detailed in Chapter 5.) Many other mindfulness-based therapies got modeled to one extent or another after MBSR.

- *Dialectical Behavior Therapy* (DBT), developed in the early 1990s by Marsha Linehan, is a treatment modality using mindfulness as a core skill for treating borderline personality disorder. It has now been expanded to treat many other disorders.

- *Mindfulness-Based Eating Awareness Training* (MB-EAT), developed by Jean Kristeller, PhD, is used to treat people with binge eating disorders or obesity.

- *Mindfulness-Based Art Therapy* is used with breast cancer patients to facilitate the release and expression of feelings.

- *Mindfulness-Based Relapse Prevention*, developed in the by G.A. Marlatt and J.R. Gordon, focuses on the prevention of relapse by substance abusers. This program uses a protocol called "urge surfing," which has individuals notice with a sense of curiosity how cravings are temporary and change in intensity moment-by-moment.

- *Mindfulness-Based Cognitive Therapy* (MBCT), developed by cognitive therapists Zindel Segal, Mark Williams, and John Teasdale, is an 8-week training program designed primarily to prevent relapses in the treatment of depression. Developed decades after Dr. Kabat-Zinn's MBSR program, it has been shown to be effective in helping depression patients to realize that their moods and thoughts are transient and impermanent, not a truth or reality.

- *Acceptance and Commitment Therapy* (ACT), developed by Steven Hayes and colleagues, is a therapy approach that has been evaluated in over 30 studies for a variety of conditions, including smoking cessation, depression, anxiety, diabetes management, and addiction. This approach expands on the cognitive-behavioral tradition by not trying to change feelings and thoughts, but rather, to emphasize the concepts of acceptance, values, mindfulness, and commitment to action.

These are just a few examples of how mindfulness can be adapted for use in healthcare. Mindfulness has also made an impact in the world of business and manufacturing, where coping with stress and burnout are major factors affecting absenteeism and productivity. These concepts will be described in more detail in Chapter 4.

MINDFULNESS AND THE TRUTH OF CHANGE

Let us return to the ancient four foundations of mindfulness mentioned above. Right now, this is the time to put a toe (or two) into the mindfulness waters. In the following experience, you'll explore what is called *anicca*, the Pali word for impermanence—which is considered to be one of the marks of existence. Then there's the wisdom that comes from realizing the truth of impermanence, which in Sanskrit is *sampajañña*, or clear knowing. As you'll see, it is this deeper knowing that helps us understand how to act in a more compassionate and intentional way.

If you've ever had an appliance that went on the fritz and fell apart, you are already well acquainted with impermanence! In terms of mindfulness, impermanence teaches us how to approach each day. That's because it illustrates that trying to grasp or hold onto anything is ultimately unsatisfying. That new car, that new job, or that new relationship cannot exactly be the same today as it was yesterday. The desire to keep your life static is futile. If you fear losing your job, losing your money, losing your partner, losing your health—that will produce what?—a lot of fear! If you want to understand change, just watch a river. The water is constantly flowing and transforming moment by moment.

Knowing the truth of impermanence at a deep level can free us from the unhappiness that comes from wanting things to be a certain way. Even if we attain any particular goal or state of mind, it will change anyway, won't it? I'm not saying to give up on your goals, but that to be rigidly stuck on them without a willingness to see things as forever transforming, is to invite unhappiness, suffering and dissatisfaction. On the other hand, it is through an acceptance of the impermanent nature of things that we can better appreciate this precious, fleeting moment—just as it is. Let's use the practice below to peer into the nature of impermanence and change.

EXPERIENCE: EXPLORING IMPERMANENCE

Take as much time as you need to follow along with the following instructions and reflections.

Part 1: Look around your surroundings and pick out one item in your environment, such as a chair, a table, a piece of clothing.

Reflect inwardly on the following:

- How permanent is the object you observed? Was it always in this form? What did it look like before it got processed? (For example, a table was once a tree, and a car was originally iron ore and petroleum products that make up its frame and the plastic parts.)

PART 2: IMAGINE THAT YOU COULD PENETRATE THE OBJECT DOWN to its molecules and atoms, seeing how it existed before it "turned into" what it is now.

Reflect on your experience with penetrating awareness:

- *How did it feel to notice things in this way? Name at least two objects that have changed in appearance since you bought them (either due to an accident, aging, exposure to the weather, etc.)*

- *What is it like to notice even your thoughts and moods as impermanent events, flowing along like the thousands of droplets that form a river?*

WHAT'S NEXT:

Congratulations on this exploration. As you go through your day, you may start to notice the changing nature of phenomena —and how this makes each moment precious and unique.

DEFINING THE MINDFULNESS ROAD MAP

There is no single, agreed upon definition of mindfulness. Many have tried to boil down the concept to a sentence or two, but that is only a moving target that changes the more you learn and experience mindfulness. Consider the mindfulness vocabulary and terminology offered here as a two-dimensional map for the real, many-dimensional experience; it is a starting point for your actual practice.

This is not to diminish the importance of the map because directions can be extremely useful when you're trying to find your way home! As you work your way through *Simply Mindful* you may want to return to this section to see how these "maps" match up with the actual terrain you are covering. In addition, give yourself permission to expand upon the vocabulary so that you can describe mindfulness in your own words and in ways that are useful to others. Here then, are a few ways of understanding mindfulness:

- Many use the idea that mindfulness is the process of noticing and calming the internal chaos of the "monkey mind"—thoughts that are jumping from one place to another. When the mind is no longer careening from future worries to past regrets, space opens for compassion and acceptance and an inner control to emerge and form a foundation for healing that breaks old behavior patterns.
- Professor Jon Kabat-Zinn, a pioneer in using mindfulness for stress reduction at the University of Massachusetts Medical School, defines mindfulness as "an open-hearted acceptance of this moment."[2]
- Meditation master and author Joseph Goldstein describes mindfulness as "the quality of paying full attention to the moment, opening to the truth of change."[3]
- From a Tibetan Buddhist perspective, Lama Surya Das, one of the first Americans to become an authorized lama, blends the ancient wisdom tradition of mindfulness with American pragmatism in his definition that emphasizes a dynamic process. Mindful change occurs, he maintains, through "the four Rs of recognition, restraint, release, and reconditioning. I developed that from thinking about how things arise, by looking at stimulus-response problems. It's good for anger management and mindful eating management. It's about attacking the root of desire and aversion, of any kind of activity [by which the mind reacts] for or against."[4]
- By contrast, Burmese meditation master Sayadaw U Pandita describes mindfulness as a deep awareness of body, sensations, mind, and emotions. What is more, this is an awareness that comes with impartiality. Because mindfulness doesn't take sides, the mind

notices all events objectively, even depression, anger, frustration, and knows them to be transient states. Mindfulness should not be passive, according to this view, but rather "dynamic, persistent, and confrontative" in its approach to breaking negative patterns. Mindfulness is dynamic because it is adaptable and flexible to each changing moment; it is persistent because the attention on an object of mind is constant and not easily distracted; it is confrontative because it neither avoids nor indulges in objects, but faces them with neutrality and objectivity.[5]

- Psychologists and Buddhist practitioners Shauna Shapiro and Linda Carlson, the authors of *The Art and Science of Mindfulness,* write that, "at the deepest level, mindfulness is about freedom: freedom from reflexive patterns, freedom from reactivity, and, ultimately, freedom from suffering."[6]

- According to Vietnamese monk, teacher and author Thich Nhat Hanh, mindfulness helps us experience "interbeing"—the truth of our connectedness to all things. In this sense, mindfulness is much more than bringing awareness to the mind and feelings and body sensations. Mindfulness dissolves the illusion of separateness and shows how everyone—and everything—is related at the most profound and deepest level. For this reason, authentic mindfulness is always grounded in taking an ethical approach to life that avoids actions that may cause harm to oneself or others.

- In Japan and China, there is both a symbol and a word that blend the essence of *now, heart,* and *mind.* This wonderful expression of mindfulness is represented by the word *nian,* and the symbol 念.

I hope that gives you a broader picture of mindfulness. Again, you needn't remember any of these "maps." They are here as touchstones that will inform the experiential practices in *Simply Mindful*. You can always come back later and take another look to see how your experience matches up with these concepts and descriptions.

In the bigger picture, mindfulness is like living each unfolding moment as an improvisation, without needing to follow an out-of-date predetermined script.

Improvisation also means letting go of trying to anticipate or control the future. Truly, we can fight and resist the way things are in this moment, or we can participate in its unfolding, with an essence of awe, grace and wonder. This may help explain why mindfulness is often described as embracing the moment-by-moment process rather than being focused on the future outcome.

Living on Purpose and Ready to Improvise

There is one additional element that was implied, but not specifically included in the above-mentioned definitions of mindfulness: Intentionality. This core aspect of mindfulness is what gives us the ability to engage conscious and purposeful living. Each intention (or lack of) ultimately shapes who we become. Intention is an essential tool to have close at hand in your mindfulness toolbox.

You might think of intention as serving the same purpose as the steering wheel in your car. If you take your hands off the wheel (we're referring to non-autonomous vehicles!), the car will drift off the road or onto oncoming traffic. The same dangerous thing happens when your attention goes elsewhere, such as texting while driving or taking your eyes off the road. Conscious intention can be viewed as a three-step process:

1) Mentally setting an intention to do a particular thing, such as to speak, move, or pay attention. This is conscious and purposeful, as opposed to randomly letting other things grab your attention (and intention), like a pop-up window on your computer screen or an ad on your phone or TV.

2) Following up by taking the desired action.

3) Observing and experiencing each action completely.

When applied like this, mindfulness establishes purposeful and present-oriented awareness. Living on purpose means that you are fully present with each unfolding moment and less likely to experience accidents and mishaps—whether physical or emotional. We do a lot of spectating in life, but intention enhances full participation living, where you are devoted 100% to whatever experience you are doing, whether washing the dishes, getting the mail, or having a conversation with a friend.

The thousands of intentions that you take in a lifetime can either be made consciously and thoughtfully, or simply be the product of mindless reactivity, habit and auto-pilot. I'm reminded of someone who once commented, "By some accident I've become the person I am." That might be true if you're not paying attention to your intentions!

Once while leading a weekly mindfulness and meditation class, I noticed that one of the attendees came to class with a large bandage covering her thumb. When I asked what happened, she told the class this story:

I was making a salad, chopping vegetables when my mind got distracted. I was thinking about something else and lost track of where my thumb was in relation to the knife!

Often, accidents happen when we're not paying attention. In this context, mindfulness can be thought of as a way of being present, on purpose, with whatever it is you are doing. As you master intention, you'll gain greater ability to turn off those anxiety-provoking news programs and raging blogs, as well as avoid impulsive eating and shopping. Eventually, you'll experience a fulfillment that comes from having greater control and being more purposeful and thoughtful about your choices.

EXPERIENCE: MOVING WITH MOMENT-BY-MOMENT INTENTION

Find a quiet place where you can practice for up to 5-minutes. (Turn off your phone or put it in airplane mode and use it as a stopwatch.)

For the next five minutes, give yourself total permission to do whatever you want. You can stand up, get a bite to eat, walk around the room, make a cup of tea, or pet the cat. *The only difference is that you will specifically set an intention before doing each action.*

If, for example, you are sitting and want to stand, you notice all the small intentions that are necessary—such as moving forward in your chair, leaning your torso forward, and lifting up with the legs. Set intentions for each movement. As you push up with your legs, know that you are pushing up. Devote yourself 100 percent to the experience of standing!

Likewise, when you take a step, make that step intentional. You can walk at a normal pace, but be aware of how each step requires the lifting of each foot, the bending of the knee, the forward movement of the leg, and the downward movement as the foot presses onto the floor. Even when you turn in a new direction, mentally say the words "turning, turning," as your body follows through and you observe each movement. What a wonderful way to gently discipline that "puppy dog" mind that likes to wander freely.

After the five minutes are up, intentionally return to your starting location. Then, set the intention to lift up *Simply Mindful*, and as you do so, pay attention to the texture, weight, temperature and shape of the book in your hands.

Practice for 5-Minutes.

Reflection on Five Minutes of Moment-to-Moment Intention:

- *What did you find as you followed each intention with an action? How present were you as you did each little thing? How different was this from how you normally move about?*

- *What was it like to be fully present with each step while walking? Did that help you appreciate your balance and how many gifts and abilities the body possesses?*

WHAT'S NEXT:

The next time you feel distracted or mentally drained, try setting intentions. We will work more with intention, but for now you can introduce this practice into your day by slowing down and being 100% present with whatever it is you're doing. You may even start appreciating the little, in-between moments that often go unnoticed.

21ST CENTURY ANTIDOTE FOR STRESS

Stress is implicated in many 21st century diseases. The American Psychological Association's Stress in America survey, for example, reveals that two of every three persons experiences either a physical or psychological symptom of stress. The plethora of symptoms includes gastric issues, insomnia, high blood pressure, anxiety, depression, and more. With that in mind, consider the following:

- Stress impairs judgment and decision-making skills.
- It helps to create or exacerbate conditions of depression, anxiety, addictions and personality disorders.
- It undermines the immune system and contributes to a range of health problems from hypertension to neurodegeneration.
- It damages relationships and distorts perceptions of life.
- Of the ten most commonly prescribed medications in the U.S., eight of them are prescribed to treat stress-related disorders.

Stress and our perceptions of stress even affect us at the cellular level to accelerate the process of aging. In a pioneering study that looked at mothers with chronically ill children, the Nobel Prize winning cellular biologist Elizabeth Blackburn and psychologist Elissa Epel found that the mothers' telomeres, located at the ends of DNA that help to hold the cell together, had been shortened by both stress and perceived stress in caring for their ill children. The dwindling of telomeres is one of the primary causes of aging, and stressed out moms had up to ten years of extra aging in their blood cells. Only those mothers who successfully maintained a positive attitude and could mentally detach from the stresses of child care were able to keep their telomeres healthy.[7]

When a stress response occurs in the body due to a stressful event, a release of hypothalamic, pituitary and adrenal hormones occurs. Cortisol and adrenaline, along with norepinephrine, wash throughout the body and the brain, resulting in such physical symptoms as accelerated heart beat, increased blood pressure, upset to the bowels and stomach. Much research has been done showing that elevated cortisol levels are linked to memory impairment, obesity, and other imbalances.

Typically, cortisol gets removed from the body after a stressful event. However, when someone experiences long-term or chronic stress, the body's high cortisol load produces serious negative effects. Cortisol actually dampens the immune system, reducing the body's T-cell count and even reducing the body's Natural Killer (NK) cells. These NK cells are important immune system cells because they fight viruses and even some kinds of cancer.

Chronic stress also impairs learning. That's because, when cortisol remains in the brain for several days, it actually kills neurons in the hippocampus—that part of the brain that helps form new memories. Cortisol not only inhibits new learning, but has been shown to make the retrieval of memories difficult.

Mindfulness practices are "a core skill necessary to help us begin to escape the vicious cycle of stress," concluded psychotherapist Richard O'Connor in his book, *Undoing Perpetual Stress.* He points out how "our nervous systems are not built for the stresses of the 21st century," and "just as our brains and nervous systems are vulnerable to the damage of stress, we have the power to heal that damage by making deliberate choices about how we live."[8]

The non-pharmaceutical, all-natural antidote to stress is mindfulness, which O'Connor says, can enable us to "literally rewire our own brains... mindfulness is a revolution in the brain, a huge change in how we think, feel, and see the world."

It's not the stressful event itself that causes us harm, so much as it is our *perception of stress*.

If you recognize that a stressor is temporary or imperманent, or if you can use your problem-solving skills to manage or work around the stress, it won't impact your body in the same negative way. This is why mindfulness helps with stress. Cultivating a curious, non-judging attitude helps us not to react as strongly to stressors, but to see them in a more neutral way—even as a learning experience that can help us overcome stressors the future.

GOOD NEWS: MINDFULNESS REWIRES THE BRAIN

Mindfulness helps to strengthen the area of the brain behind the eye brow ridge, known as the prefrontal cortex. This is perhaps the most human and integrative part of the brain. It's responsible for allowing metacognition, which is the ability to reflect inwardly on our thoughts and experiences. In addition, the prefrontal cortex is involved in empathy and feeling safe and connected to others.

The brain is so adaptable that it can create new neural networks in ways previously not thought possible. What follows are *6 Brain Myths and 6 Mindful Brain Views* that I have put together to illustrate this point.

> *BRAIN MYTH 1: Neurons cannot divide like other cells in the body. Therefore, the brain cells you are born with do not change. When brain cells die, these are never replaced.*

—**MINDFUL BRAIN VIEW**: The adult brain adds brain cells at all ages. This occurs as neural stem cells migrate up from the brain stem to centers in the brain where new learning takes place. For example, when you learn something from reading this material today, your brain creates as many as 6,000 new neurons.

> *BRAIN MYTH 2: The brain is only shaped by experiences produced by outside events or activities.*

An accomplished violinist, for example, actually changes the brain's motor cortex—enlarging the brain's physical areas devoted to the fingers and hand because of the exercise of those body parts. The brain itself cannot be changed by the mind or by thoughts.

—**MINDFUL BRAIN VIEW**: We now know that brain changes can be generated by purely internal mental activity. The work of obsessive-compulsive disorder (OCD) specialist Jeffrey Schwartz, as detailed in his book *Brain Lock*, proves that intentional and willful thought can alter the brain's physical wiring and pathways. For example, simply thinking and imagining oneself to be playing the piano leads to a measurable change in the brain's motor cortex—thus the effectiveness of cognitive and mindfulness-based therapy. In *Brain Lock*, Schwartz uses a 4-part mindfulness approach to rewiring brain networks and reducing obsessive-compulsive behaviors. This approach helps patients observe the brain's faulty signals, and lets them respond by stating, "It's not me, it's my OCD."[9]

BRAIN MYTH 3: Structures in the brain are fixed. The visual cortex can only process signals from the optic nerve. Furthermore, the sensory cortex can only process five senses.

—**MINDFUL BRAIN VIEW**: Brain "structures" are not fixed. Neurons seem to be capable of processing any information if the original pathway intended for those neurons is not used. For example, the visual cortex neurons fire in those who are non-sighted, helping them process sound as well as touch. Studies have also reported that the visual cortex can process language, a complex cognitive function. This means that the brain's initial method for processing information is "suggested" and not fixed.

> **BRAIN MYTH 4:** *What you pay attention to has absolutely no effect on the physical brain. If an area on your hand is constantly stimulated, for instance, the neuron area of the brain devoted to processing that feeling will be activated and increased— whether or not you pay attention to it.*

—**MINDFUL BRAIN VIEW**: Attention increases neuronal activity. In fact, the brain gets wired by what is in the field of focused attention. If someone is listening to music and having their hand stroked at the same time, changes in the brain only occur in those areas where that person is paying attention. This means that—for good or bad—your brain is shaped by what you choose to pay attention to.

> **BRAIN MYTH 5:** *The brain can process multiple things at once.*

—**MINDFUL BRAIN VIEW:** While we have the impression that the brain can do two things at once, like driving and talking on the cell phone, the brain shuts down one of the functions briefly while we are taking on the other task. Informational bottlenecks, or "dual task interference" that delays brain function can occur with even simple tasks—such as pressing a button at the same time a visual stimulus appears. Brain researcher Clifford Nass, a Professor of Communications at Stanford University makes this point when he says, "Multitaskers are lousy at multitasking."[10]

> **BRAIN MYTH 6:** *The brain has an affective "set point," or emotional tone that may change*

temporarily, but eventually returns to its "normal" set point. Taking this perspective, if someone's "normal" set point is being frequently unhappy or dissatisfied, nothing can change that. Long-term states of joy, happiness, and compassion are neither attainable, nor real.

—**MINDFUL BRAIN VIEW**: The brain's affective set point is not fixed and can be "re-set" over the long-term. Specific brain states related to feelings of peace, calm, optimism, and happiness are measurable. Meditation and mindfulness increase activity in parts of the brain related to focused attention, wisdom, patience, optimism, and compassion.

There's no need to remember these mindful brain views. It's enough to know that the brain is extremely fluid and adaptable, and mindfulness helps reshape the brain in ways that help you to better cope with that roller coaster known as life.

Detoxifying Stress

Our day-to-day experiences of life influence our stress hormone levels, observes Emma K. Adam of Northwestern University's Center on Social Disparities and Health, and in turn, those stress hormone levels directly influence our experience of daily living. She and three research colleagues took saliva samples three times a day for three consecutive days from 156 older adults born between 1935 and 1952.[11] Adults who experienced feelings of loneliness the night before invariably had higher cortisol levels the next morning when they awoke. The same elevation was true if they felt sadness, lack of control, or being threatened when they went to sleep. It's as if the body knows it needs to prepare for another stressful day.

Another study, this one in *Psychosomatic Medicine*, looked at cortisol levels in 66 teachers from public schools by sampling saliva on three consecutive days, starting at the time when they awoke. Teachers who scored high on perceived stress and burnout showed a higher overall cortisol secretion each morning, and they also measured the lowest levels of self-esteem, the highest external locus of control, and the greatest number of somatic complaints of any subgroup of teachers studied.[12]

Studies like these show that we can't always control the stresses in our lives. However, with practices like the one that follows, we can discharge stress and soothe ourselves as needed. That is why the 3-Minute Stress Detox exercise below is one of the most important exercises that I can offer you.

You can take these detox breaks anytime, but especially during times of uncertainty and transitions in your life. You can use the breaks just before and after driving your vehicle, before a meeting, even while standing in a line. Take one of these breaks at least once a morning even when you don't think you need it.

This exercise is useful because it is totally portable and potent.

EXPERIENCE: 3-MINUTE MINDFUL STRESS DETOX

When first practicing, find a quiet space where you won't be disturbed.

For the next three minutes, you will learn how to reduce the accumulation of stress that can quickly build up during the day.

As you do this, you will be focusing on three basic things—body, breath, and identifying any tension or emotion. (***Note, if you feel distressed at any time, you can stop and try again later if need be.***)

MINUTE #1: FOR 60-SECONDS, NOTICE YOUR POSTURE AND BODY. Right now, sit up erect, letting yourself find a posture that allows you to breathe easily.

For a few seconds, notice how your feet rest firmly on the floor. Get the sense that your body is being supported, almost elevated, by the ground and the Earth. Let yourself feel the sense of poise and grace that this position gives you.

Minute #2: For the next 60-seconds, place your attention on the breath. Observe the length of each in-breath and out-breath. Find a normal rhythm of breathing that is dynamic, natural, and free. Do not try to force your breath. It matters not if the breath is long or short. Just know that *it's perfect just as it is*! You might imagine how each breath rises and falls like a balloon that expands then shrinks. As you exhale, release with a long, slow and satisfying breath.

Minute #3: For the last 60-seconds, watch for any tension, tightness, or emotions residing in your body. If there's an emotion, just name whatever it is—such as sadness, anger, hurt, impatience, etc. Then, you will use your imagination to visualize a white or golden light entering in from the crown of the head as you inhale. Let this light be drawn into the tension-filled part of your body and filling it up completely. With each exhale, visualize the light as it carries all the impurities or negative emotions down through the legs and out through the bottom of your feet—where they are deposited back into the earth for recycling. As you do this, let that part of the body grow softer and more relaxed.

Reflection on the 3-minute Stress Detox:

- *What was this stress detox like for you? Were you able to notice areas of tension and emotions? Just do your best to give any emotion a name. (Naming emotions has been shown to help quiet down the stress part of the brain.)*

- *When can you use a stress detox break? How can you work this into your day?*

WHAT'S NEXT:

If this is a new practice, give it time and be patient with yourself. As with any focused practice, it's normal for thoughts, sounds, memories, or sensations to temporarily attract your attention. Notice them, but gently return to your breath and three-step process If you don't feel any tension, just breathe naturally, sensing the calming rhythm of breath.

In Chapter 2, you'll work with variations of mindful breathing meditation practices.

∾

KEY CHAPTER REFERENCES

1. Langer, E.J. Moldoveanu, M. (2000) The Construct of Mindfulness. *Journal of Social Issues.* 56; 1:1-9.

2. Kabat-Zinn, Jon. (2006) *Coming to Our Senses: Healing Ourselves and the World Through Mindfulness.* New York: Hyperion.

3. Goldstein, Joseph. (2003) *Insight Meditation.* Boston: Shambhala.

4. Altman, Donald. Author interview with Lama Surya Das. January, 11, 2006.

5. Pandita, S.U. (1992) *In This Very Life.* Boston: Wisdom Publications.

6. Shapiro, S.L., Carlson, L.E. (2009) *The Art and Science of Mindfulness.* Washington, D.C.: American Psychological Association.

7. Epel E., Blackburn E. et. al. (2004) Accelerated Telomere Shortening in Response to Life Stress. *Proceedings of the National Academy of Sciences.* www.pnas.org/content/101/49/17312.full.

8. O'Connor, R. (2005) *Undoing Perpetual Stress.* New York: Berkley Books.

9. Schwartz, J. (2016) *Brain Lock: Free Yourself from Obsessive-Compulsive Behavior.* New York: Harper Perennial.

10. Gorlick, A. (2009) Media multitaskers pay mental price, Stanford study shows. Stanford University News Service.

11. Adam, E.K., et al. (2006) Day-to-Day dynamics of experiences—cortisol associations in a population-based sample of older adults. *Proceedings of the National Academy of Sciences.* 2006 Nov 7; 103(45):17058-17063.

12. Pruessner, J.C., et al. (1999) Burnout, Perceived Stress, and Cortisol Responses to Awakening. *Psychosomatic Medicine.* 1999; 61:197-204.

2

SECRETS OF THE ORGANIC HERE AND NOW

*D*egree by degree, we humans probably don't notice how our core attentional awareness abilities are being slowly stripped away by the technological convergence of increased speed and demands on our time. We're barraged by the insatiable need for more and more technology. Instead of leaving us with more time, we are left with less. For many, their response is to seek escape through lifestyle addictions or be driven to distraction through multitasking. But going on autopilot and acting out compulsive and addictive behaviors or to attempt multitasking is not the answer.

If you think you are a great multitasker, you may be surprised to learn about what it does to the brain. Three Stanford University researchers tested the proposition that students can effectively perform a high-tech juggling act of multitasking, such as sending emails or text messages while trying to study or watch a television program. A group of 100 students were put through a series of three tests. Researchers developed a media multi-tasking index questionnaire to distinguish heavy media multitaskers (HMM) from light media multi-taskers (LMM). According to the study, the baseline for media use was based on "the mean number of media a person simultaneously consumes."[1]

Was there a cognitive price that HMMs paid for their attempts to split attention and concentration? It turned out that there was, and the price was steep. In fact, the chronic HMMs couldn't keep information separate in their minds. They couldn't filter out irrelevant information or organize their memories effectively. On all three tests the HMMs underperformed compared to the LMMs. "When they're in situations where there are multiple sources of information coming from the external world or emerging out of memory, they're not able to filter out what's not relevant to their current goal," observed one of the study's authors, Anthony D. Wagner, an associate professor of psychology. "That failure to filter means they're slowed down by that irrelevant information."[2]

It is my belief that critical wiring in the brain for interpersonal relationships is also being short-circuited by this fixation on multi-tasking and the barrage of sensory and media assaults on core awareness. Our attention is being splintered and fragmented, and the prefrontal cortex—that "reflect and relate" part of the brain responsible for enhancing face-to-face, personal contact and genuine interpersonal dialogue—is being sacrificed on the altar of time and speed consolidation. Direct personal contact is being replaced by text messaging and emailing, where the potential for meaningful exchanges is low and the potential for misunderstandings is high.

Basic mindfulness practice provides a resource for enhanced concentration and focus, a higher quality of empathy and compassion in relationships, and a path to giving one's experience of life more meaning through a greater appreciation of the little things in daily existence that matter.

If there truly were a secret to accessing the organic here and now, the well-known 20th century spiritual teacher Krishnamurti illuminated it with these words:

*Truth can never wither because it can
only be found from moment to moment
in every thought, in every relationship,
in every word, in every gesture,
in a smile, in tears.*[3]

INTENTIONALLY CENTERING ATTENTION NOW

I have created a term to describe the four activating qualities of the living and dynamic awareness that is mindfulness. The term *Intentionally Centering Attention Now*, or I-CAN, will help you understand the process of this particular quality of mind. As you continue to deepen your own practice and exploration of mindfulness as described in these pages, you can refer back to this chapter as a way to interpret your experiences.

The "I" in I-CAN stands for *intention*. You might think of intention as the engine of effort. It is with intention that you decide what to bring into your life. It is through intention that you follow the values, purpose, and vision that matter to you. Intention is a powerful and primary agent of change that is necessary to break old habits and addictions.

The second quality of I-CAN, *centering*, helps you respond to stress—be it internal or external stressors—with an attitude of acceptance and openness. Centering encourages a more spacious, compassionate and non-judgmental attitude toward life, from one's daily emotions and experiences to one's inner dialogue. In this way you can develop a greater sense of flow, equanimity, and hope. Of course, centering does not guarantee that difficult situations won't occur, but it can foster a greater sense of acceptance of life as it is.

The third characteristic of I-CAN, *attention*, has to do with sharpening the mind's innate faculties for concentration. Without a high quality of attention, it is difficult to maintain the level attention needed to focus on or observe things deeply. When you contact anything—are you able to confront it with strong and determined observational power? Are you able to meet it with curiosity and openness—without being distracted, attracted, repulsed, or confused?

Remember, too, that attention is a basic and valuable life skill that is required for finding resources or completing most jobs. Attention is also essential for reflecting, contemplating, and seeking wisdom. The more you cultivate attention, the more of a discerning buffer you have from the constant barrage of media seeking to win your precious attention.

The last quality of mindfulness as found in I-CAN is the *now*. The now captures your sense of participation in life. It makes you feel awake and alive. Only in the now can you be totally flexible with thought and action as each moment unfolds. This makes it possible to escape the gravity that pulls you toward unhealthy habits, cravings, or mental scripts that filter out the now. The more you engage these catalyzing properties of mindfulness— intention, centering, attention, and presence in the now —the more you will find fresh, energizing and liberating ways of relating to your daily experiences.

CAPTURING THE NOW

There are profoundly different kinds of awareness that can be used to connect with this moment. Bear in mind that the kind of awareness you apply can make the difference between addictive behaviors and balanced ones. To better understand these different kinds of awareness, let's engage the use of a metaphor. Imagine that basic awareness is like a light that shines outward onto various objects, and when that light reflects back to us we come into contact with that object.

Through your senses, basic everyday awareness contacts various objects that exist in the Now Moment—whether through sight, sound, taste, touch, smell. Not only do your senses directly contact objects, but the mind further deciphers these experiences by how it perceives and thinks about them. As you can imagine, this is a very personal process, and that's why any experience—whether seeing a sunset to tasting an orange— is different for everyone.

This process can be shown by the illustration below. Basic awareness mediates not only your outer world, but also your inner mental world of thoughts, memories, beliefs, etc.—which is why such mental interpretations as "I must be having a panic attack" or "I'm always inept," have the power to affect us physically and emotionally. However, as you're about to discover in the following experience, there are other mediating factors that shape just how this contact is made.

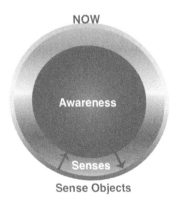

EXPERIENCE: NOTICING FOR 3-MINUTES

Read the instructions below, and then practice this short meditation.

For three minutes, look around the room, or environment, that you are in as you read this. Simply use the sense door of vision to notice whatever is around you. If you have thoughts or feelings about these objects and colors, that is okay. If you are attracted or repulsed by something, just follow your impulse. Don't try to block anything out. Look at any objects for as long as you want.

Practice for 3-Minutes.

Reflection on Noticing:

- *While looking around, what thoughts or feelings did you notice—pleasant or unpleasant or neutral—about any particular objects, shapes or colors?*

- *How long did you tend to gaze at objects that grabbed your attention?*

- *Did you get distracted at any point—by a sound, memory, thought, or sensation? (See if you can remember what distracted you.)*

WHAT'S NEXT:
You just contacted a lot of objects with your awareness. After reading the following text, you'll be ready for another short, but very different awareness practice.

GOING BEYOND BASIC AWARENESS
When an untrained mind—or what could be considered to be an undiscriminating awareness—contacts sense objects in

the way you just experienced, there may be narrow awareness and limited choice as to how the objects are experienced and confronted.

Imagine someone with an untamed mind and a history of emotional eating sees a chocolate bar during a period of high stress. This individual will be confronted by multiple streams of awareness that appear as desires, cravings, memories, conditioning and impulses. It will be almost impossible to view that chocolate bar in an objective and neutral way. That's just one example of how we can get overwhelmed by sense objects. (If you've been on a diet or struggled with any kind of addiction you know what I mean.) The constant push and pull of inner impulses can leave one feeling overwhelmed and defeated. Fortunately, a trained mind can overcome previous conditioning, giving anyone the capacity to step back, pause and review alternative options to that chocolate bar—even during a period of high stress.

Continuing with the earlier metaphor of basic awareness as a light that can contact any object, suppose that there is now a *second light* that is located *inside* the first light of basic awareness. This second light **illuminates basic awareness,** so it can watch everything that basic awareness does—how it operates, what it is drawn to, what conditioned behaviors it follows and how it goes on auto-pilot. It notices doubt, listens in on conflicting inner dialogue, witnesses how thoughts and emotions arise and fall away. This second inner light is like a bare awareness and wakefulness that is always on, always present—even if you are not consciously aware of it. When you learn to access it, it becomes a powerful mediator of your experience. No longer are you driven by basic awareness because you clearly see the inner workings and phenomena as they occur in the mind, moment by moment.

Thoughts can be subtle and the roots and causes of conditioned behavior are not always obvious. As the Tibetan teacher and author Lama Surya Das explains, "You are aware of the button pusher. And you recognize 'There, it is happening again.'"[4] As shown in the illustration, innersight illuminates all the processes of awareness that were previously hidden. Because mindfulness activates innersight, it opens the way for contacting the here and now in a more complete, intentional, open and neutral way.

I have coined the term *innersight* to describe this unfettered awareness. It has no agenda other than to just *be*. This inner light is bare consciousness, so it simply notices things without coloring them or adding or subtracting any thoughts or judgments onto an experience. *Innersight* is represented by the innermost circle in the following illustration.

EXPERIENCE: NOTICING THE NON-JUDGMENTAL
NOW FOR 3-MINUTES

Read the instructions and then practice this brief meditation.

You will once again use the sense door of vision to observe your surroundings. The difference this time is that you will not gaze on anything for more than a second or two. You will use your eyes to scan, and as you do so, try not to look at entire objects, but notice the fine and small details, colors, textures, and shapes within an object—as if you are seeing these for the first time.

Keep your eyes moving so your mind doesn't have time to put a label or a name on these objects. Likewise, let yourself notice these shapes and colors with an attitude of neutrality and non-judgment. For example, the colors blue or red or green are not innately good or bad. They are just that color.

If you notice your mind commenting, just notice the thoughts and return to the scanning.

Practice for 3-minutes.

Reflection on Noticing the Non-Judgmental Now:

- *How different was this than seeing things with "normal" awareness?*

- *What did it feel like to notice, without adding mental filters, perceptions and judgements such as "like," "dislike," "beautiful," etc.*

- *During those moments when you were fully participating 100% in observing with vision, where were your thoughts?*

WHAT'S NEXT:

Congratulations on contacting awareness in a fresh, more neutral way. As you go through your day, this practice can help you begin to notice how quickly the mind quickly adds a judging filter to most objects.

GRAVITY FREE AWARENESS

I like to think of innersight as gravity free awareness, because it's an awareness that is not stuck in the orbit of the ego's needs, desires or past conditioning. This is what makes it spacious and free floating. Further, innersight has two important properties, or characteristics:

- **Innersight lets you contact and participate in the now moment as it occurs, instead of being hooked into old scripts about the past or worries about the future.**

- **Innersight increases your capacity to consciously transform basic awareness into a form of selective, high quality attention.**

For these reasons, *innersight* promotes a more non-judgmental and open mindset when encountering persons and situations—even those difficult persons in your life. Innersight is always there, but keep in mind that it takes some work to get past the blockade of multiple input streams of memories, perceptions, and conditioning that keep us from accessing its liberating light.

With practice, you'll begin to notice those times that the mind quickly grabs onto objects or habits of thought that you might *not* want to maintain, or hold onto—such as a negative belief or perception. By witnessing the truth of the moment, you are more able to engage conscious intention to get unstuck and move attention elsewhere. This is one way to maintain emotional balance and shift awareness to the unfiltered, joy-filled moment.

KEY PRACTICES OF BASIC MINDFULNESS

Simply Mindful uses the following practices to steep you in the present moment, instill feelings of tranquility, and develop innersight so that you can find joy and peace on a more consistent basis.

Mindful Breathing—active breathing engages conscious control over inhalation and exhalation, as opposed to passive or 'normal' breathing. Active diaphragmatic breathing involves controlling the way air is drawn into the lungs through the nose or mouth by regulating the depth of breath, the time it is held in the lungs, and the rate at which the air is released.

This means full awareness as breath occurs. For example, if breathing a short breath, know that this is a short breath; if breathing a long breath, know that this is a long breath. The average person takes approximately 18,000-20,000 breaths each day. Bringing even a handful of breaths into full awareness can profoundly alter one's emotional and physical well-being.

Body Scan—a method of developing non-judgmental, neutral awareness by placing attention on sensations as they occur in various parts of the body, moment-by-moment. As described in detail in Chapter 5, the body scan decentralizes the usual "I-centric" personalized focus, or perspective, that most people have of the body. This training lets one experience the body in a new way that creates space from various personal stories and narratives that may cause suffering and pain. This form of noticing cultivates a more neutral and objective perspective toward sensations in the body and has even been shown to decrease perception of pain.

Meditation—a practice of building and sustaining concentration, usually by focusing awareness on an object through a variety of techniques, whether placing attention on the breath, body, or mental phenomena (thoughts, memories, perceptions, etc.), or a sound, word, or image, usually with eyes closed and while sitting in a comfortable position, results in a silencing of ordinary consciousness that produces a state of restful alertness. Later in this guidebook, *Vipassanā*, or insight meditation, will be explained as a means of combining breathing and the conscious release of thoughts.

Mindful Movement—any intentional movement, such as mindful walking, allows one to practice the three-step method mentioned earlier, of 1) setting an intention, 2) following up with the action, and 3) observing and fully participating in the action.

Often, you may hear the phrase "mindfulness meditation," and that is because awareness of what is happening moment-by-moment is often combined with focused attention. Mindful breathing, for example, generates both awareness of breath in each moment as well as enhancing focus and concentration. It's worth noting that many of the exercises in this guidebook blend breathing, meditative focus, non-judgmental awareness, and moment-to-moment movement.

THE POWER OF BREATH

Breath has been so revered in human history that archeologists have recovered 4,000-year-old statues from India that depict yogic breathing positions. The Buddha's *Anapanasati sutta*, or discourse on mindfulness with breathing, has guided generations of mindfulness practitioners on how to properly use the breath as a tool for relaxing body and mind, as well as for gaining insight. Eventually, these ancient breathing practices made their way to the West.

In the 1960s, Harvard professor and cardiologist Herbert Benson investigated how breathing techniques used by practitioners of Transcendental Meditation (TM) produced a series of reactions that he called "the relaxation response."[5] At the time, mind-body medicine was neither understood nor accepted, and meditation was considered a "fringe" practice. Despite even his own initial resistance to TM, Benson's research showed that such focused breathing results in a family of beneficial psychological and physiological effects. These include:

- Lowering of blood pressure and cleansing of blood lactate levels (lactate in the blood is a chemical that creates feelings of anxiety).
- Decreasing of the heart rate, metabolism, and breathing rate.
- Increasing alpha brain waves to produce a feeling of being alert and calm at the same time.
- Increasing serotonin—a neurotransmitter that improves mood and mental flexibility.
- Overall sense of well-being and calming of the body's reactive limbic system.
- Benson's later research examined how focused awareness turns on a set of over 2,000 genes related to the immune system, free radicals in the body and aging. [6]

Diaphragmatic breathing (breathing in deeply into your belly) is a conscious and intentional way to turn on your body's relaxation system, and it only takes three of these diaphragmatic breaths or about twenty seconds. In other words, it drastically changes your body chemistry by turning down the stress response. I like to think of diaphragmatic breathing as the thermostat for the body and the brain. When your emotional systems are overheating, you can reset and cool everything down with conscious breathing.

Here's how it works. When breathing into this deepest part

of your lungs, the lungs in turn press on the diaphragmatic wall, which is the muscle that separates the chest and abdominal cavities. The pressure of the diaphragmatic wall squeezes the abdominal cavity and causes your abdomen to flatten out and expand in all directions—front, sides, and back.

Now, when the abdomen expands toward your spine, it presses on and activates the vagus nerve, which runs along the inside of your spine. Stimulation of this nerve is what turns on the body's built-in relaxation response. Shallow breathing, however, doesn't provide these same benefits. In fact, shallow breaths reinforce the body's 'flight or fight' alarm system, which causes the release of stress hormones such as cortisol and adrenaline.

Studies on the bodily impact of these hormones, especially cortisol, show how they temporarily block memory retrieval. Functional magnetic resonance imaging (fMRI) used in some studies suggest that higher cortisol levels are often associated with a stronger response in the brain's amygdala to emotionally arousing stimuli. This impairs memory retrieval—which can affect both judgment and the ability to function effectively on the job or in situations that require rapid responses.[7]

EXPERIENCE: LEARN TO BREATHE
DIAPHRAGMATICALLY

Follow along with the instructions below. By the way, we were all born as belly breathers. That's why, once you re-learn this, you'll find it to be natural and effortless.

Are you a Belly Breather or Chest Breather?

First, let's take a moment to see whether you are a chest breather, or a belly breather. To do this, begin by sitting in a chair. Next, place the palm of one hand on your chest, on top of your heart, or a little higher up. Next, place your other palm on your belly, just above your navel but below the rib cage.

Now, take several breaths. As you do this, breathe in through your nose and out through your nose or mouth, whichever feels more natural.

Which hand is moving the most?

Both hands usually move—however, if the top hand is moving more, you are probably chest breathing. But if the palm over your belly noticeably moves out and in with the breath, then you are likely breathing diaphragmatically, or belly breathing. Again, if both hands move, that's okay—just notice which one is moving more. If you are already belly breathing—then congratulations. You will still want to practice the steps below to enhance your belly breathing.

The Three Breathing Postures

You will now learn three simple postures that promote belly breathing.

Posture #1: Right now, place your arms behind your back and clasp your hands together as in the illustration below.

This movement stretches the intercostals—groups of muscles that help hinge the ribs open so it is easier to breathe in to the lungs more deeply. You can stand or sit while doing this. Take several breaths. If you feel light headed or dizzy you may be taking too deep a breath.

Do you feel a difference? Is your abdomen expanding or moving? If this is a new experience for you, allow yourself time to practice. Eventually, breathing into the belly will be natural and easy.

POSTURE #2: A SECOND WAY TO get a deeper breath is to simply place your hands at your sides. As you do this, make sure that your hands are making contact with the bottom of your ribcage. Take a few breaths, and you should feel movement and expansion at the sides of the body. Remember, that breathing occurs in three dimensions, which means your abdomen expands in the front and back, as well as at the sides of the body.

POSTURE #3: LIGHTLY CLASP YOUR HANDS behind your head or neck. If this posture is too difficult or painful, raise your arms up and just touch your fingertips to the tops of your shoulders.

For those persons who hold the stomach in, let the abdominal muscles relax during the in-breath. You might even say the word "soften" or "relaxed" as you breathe in.

Reflection on the Three Breathing Postures:

- *Which of the three postures best helped you experience and*

deepen your breathing? What did you notice in the body as
you took these deeper breaths?

- *How could you use this posture during the day to practice—*
  even for a few minutes at a time to reduce stress?

WHAT'S NEXT:

If diaphragmatic breathing is new to you, don't give up.
Over time you will train the body to relax in this way. Consider
creating breathing breaks where you can practice during the
day. In fact, the next experience will get you started.

EXPERIENCE: 3-MINUTE CALMING BREATH
PRACTICE

For this practice you will use the diaphragmatic breathing posture
from above that worked best for you.

Find a place where you won't be disturbed. Sit in an upright,
but relaxed posture. Use a timer if that helps you do this exercise. If your mind starts wandering, such as thinking about the
past or the future, simply notice this with a sense of curiosity.
Then, bring your attention back to your diaphragmatic
breathing.

Practice for 3-minutes.

Reflection on the Calming Breath Practice:

- *What did you notice as you did this practice? Was the mind*
  quieter? More focused on the breath?

- *How could you use even a 3-minute practice daily? When during your day would this be most helpful?*

WHAT'S NEXT:

Eventually, you won't need to place your hands behind your back or head in order to get a belly breath. Most importantly, practice daily or when you can to create this new relaxing and healthy habit.

To sum up, with this practice you have learned to use both a calming breath and concentrated mind practice. This brings tranquility to the body and helps the mind increase its ability to focus and concentrate. In traditional mindfulness this is called *samatha*, or a tranquility meditation, and you can use it anytime as a practice for quieting the mind and developing calm.

While you could just do the calm breathing (samatha) practice, you can also combine it with a form of meditation that activates and strengthens innersight awareness—which is traditionally called *vipassana*, or insight meditation. This works well because each form of practice enhances the other. You'll get a taste of this integrated mindfulness meditation in an upcoming experience.

THE IMPORTANCE OF INTENTIONALITY AND INSIGHT MEDITATION

As mentioned earlier in this chapter's discussion of I-CAN, bringing intentionality to your body, breath, thought, and daily activity heightens your awareness, which facilitates the ability to break free from habits. When you think about it, intentionality is how you create your life. It is the fuel for generating effort and the means by which you activate your dreams and desires.

If you doubt the power of intention, consider how every thing in your life at this moment—your car, your living arrangements, your relationships, your job situation—began as an intention. Advertisers understand the power of intentions, and they willingly pay millions of dollars for ads to turn *their* intentions into *your* intentions!

You can take charge over your own intentionality throughout your daily routine simply by making a mental note to be aware of your breathing, how you walk, sit, stand, or interact with others and your environment.

What is particularly useful about intentionality is when you use it to counter negative or limiting thoughts. For example, a possible intention might be, "I will notice how the mind creates limiting intentions. And I will be curious, not blaming, when this happens. Instead, I will refocus toward more positive affirmations, such as wishing myself and others health and happiness."

Brain research demonstrates that setting the intention to name and label your feelings and emotions can help you to calm and inhibit that reactive part of the brain. A study by J. David Creswell and colleagues had subjects view emotionally triggering photos. Those subjects who could name the emotions elicited in the photos were able to stay calm. This mechanism appears to work through the prefrontal cortex sending inhibiting signals to the amygdala, helping to quiet it down.[8]

By watching mental activity from a safe distance, you can objectively notice and label feelings—mentally stating *there's frustration, there's anger, there's hurt*, and *there's sadness*, etc. This strengthens innersight awareness, and gives you a deep understanding of how the mind works, what it is attracted to, repulsed by, and how it generates a constant stream of mental phenomena. By practicing this form of neutral observation—

what we've mentioned previously as traditional vipassana meditation—you may discover that thoughts and emotions are not as scary or as frightening as you imagined. You can even observe how mental phenomena rise and fall, just like your breath.

Intentionality and insight into the mind are skills that you can practice. In the following experience, you'll practice an integrated mindfulness meditation practice. This practice combines tranquil breathing with awareness of thoughts and mind.

EXPERIENCE: 5-MINUTE INTEGRATED MINDFUL BREATH MEDITATION (CALMING BREATH WITH INSIGHT AND INTENTIONALITY)

Find a quiet location where you can sit in a chair or a cushion with your legs crossed. Keep your back straight and find a comfortable rhythm with your breath. Read through the entire practice first, trying the different elements.

In this exercise, you will learn the basics of combining a tranquility and concentration breath practice (samatha) with a deep innersight awareness practice (vipassana). To this we'll add a simple method for breathing with intentionality.

Once you understand and have tried each of the three parts, you'll practice this integrated mindfulness meditation for five minutes.

Breathing Part 1: Anchor Point Breathing

Anchor points with the breath can change from day to day. Right now, take a few breaths and *notice the place(s) in the body where you most vividly notice the physical sensation of breath right now*—such as in the nasal passage, the throat, the movement of the chest or belly, etc. This will be today's anchor point with the breath, and it will help you keep focus as you breathe.

Remember that you will be using belly breathing as practiced earlier.

Right now, practice placing your attention on the anchor point for the duration of an entire breath—the in-breath, the pause, the out-breath.

Excellent! Now move on to Part 2.

Breathing Part 2: Observe the Mind

Even though you'll be placing awareness on the breath, your mind will inevitably wander off to something—past, future, or even a self-referential thought. That's okay, because becoming aware of mind wandering is part of training yourself to awaken to what's occurring in the mind moment-by-moment—as opposed to just getting "lost in thoughts."

When you notice the mind has drifted off from your breathing anchor point, just name this as "wandering" or "thinking." You can also name emotions if you are feeling any. If you're a visual person, you might visualize thoughts as clouds passing by in the sky or a leaf floating on a river.

The process of labeling or visualizing will help you to disengage from the mind wandering so you can gently bring your attention back to the breath and your anchor point in the body.

Right now, spend a minute or two getting to know the contents of your mind by noticing and labeling your thoughts as described above.

Wonderful. You're ready to move on to Part 3.

Breathing Part 3: Intentional Breathing

Set an Intention for Each In and Out Breath. This will give your mind a job and keep it busy noticing each breath. Here's how it works:

- With each inhalation, set an intention to breathe in by mentally stating *Creating a Breath*
- With each exhalation, set an intention to breathe out by mentally stating: *Ending a Breath*
- You could also mentally note your intention with the words "creating" and "ending" or even the words "in" and "out."
- Another useful practice is to just drop the words and just notice the sensation of "rising" and "falling" as the breath goes in and out. See what works best for you.

Right now, let's see what it is like to be 100% devoted to the experience of each breath.

For 5-minutes, do the entire mindful breathing practice of 1) placing awareness on the breath, 2) observing and releasing thoughts, and 3) being intentional with the breath.

Reflection on Integrated Breathing Practice:

- *What was the easiest thing about this integrated meditation? What was most difficult about it? How would more practice help you to get familiar with it?*

- *What was it like for you to label thoughts or emotions and release them without grabbing on?*

- *What was it like to bring intentionality to the breath?*

- *Were you more or less distracted while using intention with the breath? For many, this helps steady the mind.*

- *What challenges do I face to creating a daily practice?*

- *How many minutes of daily breath practice am I willing to commit to? When and where would I practice? How can I develop a plan that works?*

WHAT'S NEXT:

Congratulations on learning a more complete practice of getting present with the body, the breath, and the mind. Above all, remember that this is a process not an outcome, and there's no such thing as being perfect with it. Quieting the hyperactive monkey mind takes time. Be sure to invite your self-hospitality and self-kindness as you continue to practice.

Moving forward, think about setting a schedule for when you can practice integrated mindful breathing. You might even want to create a serene and sacred space where you can practice. Over time, you'll start to notice that there's a different quality of deep attention and tranquility. Above all, as you get more familiar and comfortable with a breathing practice, feel free to adapt it to fit your needs.

MEDICINE FOR THE WHOLE BEING

Breathing is probably one of the best methods you can use to practice I-CAN and care for your whole being. You pay attention to body each time that you notice the length of each breath. You can also bring awareness to how you are calming the body and reducing stress with each conscious breath.

Read the wise words, below, that the Buddha advises in his mindful breath teaching, the *Anapanasati sutta*. Remember to bring this deep awareness with you each time that you take a short, or long, mindful breath. Even this practice below is a complete mindful body-breath-mind meditation.

How inspiring!

> *When breathing in long, one knows: "I breathe in long."*
> *While breathing out long, one knows: "I breathe out long."*
> *When breathing in short, one knows: "I breathe in short." While breathing out short, one knows: "I breathe out short."*
> *One trains oneself: "Sensitive to the whole body, I breathe in. Sensitive to the whole body, I breathe out.*
> *One trains oneself: "Calming the whole body, I breathe in. Calming the whole body, I breathe out.*[9]

~

KEY CHAPTER REFERENCES

1. Gorlick, A. (2009) Media multitaskers pay mental price, Stanford study shows. Stanford University News Service. August 24, 2009.

2. Ophir, E. Nass, C. Wagner, A.D. (2009) Cognitive control in media multitaskers. *Proceedings of the National Academy of Sciences.* 2009 Sep 15: 106(37); 15583-15587.

3. Krishnamurti, J., (1995) *The Book of Life: Daily Meditations with Krishnamurti.* New York: HarperOne, p. viii.

4. Altman, Donald. Author interview with Lama Surya Das. January, 11, 2006.

5. Benson, H. (2000) *The Relaxation Response.* New York: William Morrow Paperbacks.

6. Benson, H., and Proctor, W. (2010) *Relaxation Revolution.* New York: Scribner.

7. Wolf, O.T. (2009) Stress and memory in humans: Twelve years of progress? *Brain Research.* 2009 Oct 13; 1293:142-54.

8. Creswell, J.D., Way, M., Eisenberger, N., Lieberman, M. (2007) Neural correlates of dispositional mindfulness during affect labeling. *Psychosomatic Medicine.* 69:560–565 (2007).

9. Rosenberg, Larry. (2004) *Breath by Breath: The Liberating Practice of Insight Meditation.* Boston: Shambhala.

3

ALL-NATURAL INGREDIENTS FOR
DAILY MINDFULNESS

*M*any individuals who I introduce to mindfulness often ask: How important is it to develop a daily mindfulness practice? How much mindfulness does one need to know? These questions are important for anyone dedicated to learning mindfulness. My answer is basically this: Trying to learn mindfulness skills without practicing them is much like playing an online virtual sport and believing you've actually mastered that sport.

The good news is that the mindfulness work you do is cumulative, so the more effort you put in, the greater your return. Mindfulness acts as a protective buffer and coping skill that is especially helpful when dealing with stress. In addition, since mindfulness brings heightened awareness into any activity, it is well suited for using with daily self-care activities that are sure to jump-start and maintain any mindfulness practice. These activities are what I refer to as the *Five Steps to G-R-E-A-T Mindful Self-Care.*

    Step 1 – G-ratitude
    Step 2 – R-elationships
    Step 3 – E-ating & Sleeping

Step 4 – A-ctivity

Step 5 – T-une-Up with Mindfulness

Let's take a closer look at why each of these is relevant to supporting your mindfulness practice.

MINDFUL SELF-CARE STEP 1 – GRATITUDE AND ATTITUDE

Gratitude is all about re-tuning your attitude. You might think of gratitude as a form of mental jujitsu that is powerful enough to flip a negative attitude into a positive one. Consider, for example, negative self-talk. Like it or not, everyone has to confront negative self-talk. It might be that inner voice telling you that you're not smart enough, successful enough, or that you should "be more like so-and-so." Trying to deny or run away from negativity takes a lot of energy. You might even end up in a mental war with those thoughts by trying to rationalize them away, only to have them come back even stronger. If this has happened to you, consider applying gratitude.

Before you start thinking, "Oh, yeah, that's what my grandmother used to go on and on about," let's look at some research that might surprise you. One major research project by gratitude researchers Robert Emmons and Michael McCullough, showed that a gratitude practice resulted in the following effects on well-being:

- Higher levels of life satisfaction and more optimism and vitality about life.
- Better progress toward personal goals and goal attainment.
- Reduced levels of stress and depressed mood.
- Greater level of motivating factors such as enthusiasm, energy, and determination in the face of daily activities.

- More prosocial behavior, such as helping and providing emotional support to others.
- Reduced focus on materialism as a definition of one's success, as well as fewer feelings of negative emotions such as envy toward others.
- A sample of adults with neuromuscular disease, showed "positive moods, a greater sense of feeling connected to others, more optimistic ratings of one's life, and better sleep duration and sleep quality."[1]

A study detailed by Sonja Lyubomirsky in her book, *The How of Happiness,* revealed that "the gratitude group reported significantly bigger increases in their happiness levels from before to after the intervention." It was only necessary for participants in this study to do the practice once a week, such as on a Sunday night, for the benefits to be felt.[2]

This is really just the tip of the iceberg when describing the benefits of gratitude. Another study, for example, has shown how gratitude produces prosocial behavior and assistance for others, even when there's a cost to helping. According to the study, "it can increase assistance provided to strangers."[3]

In my own practice as a psychotherapist, I've seen dramatic shifts in mood and narrative as the result of a simple gratitude intervention. Let me share my experience with Jerry (all names are changed), who had a history of family depression that stretched back generations. His grandfather had been in and out of mental hospitals for years, and his mother was diagnosed with acute depression and had trouble functioning. In Jerry's own words, "I have a genetic history of depression and there's nothing I can do about it."

But Jerry had not yet encountered the mind-bending power of gratitude. As he explored it, a major shift occurred in his outlook and life. He started asking people at work what they had gratitude for. Soon, gratitude became a touchstone that transformed his understanding and perception of events—one that represented a very different way of thinking and being in the world.

Over time, Jerry's inner narrative changed. I still recall the day he said to me, "I have periods of depression, but I know how to effectively manage them using gratitude and other skills." That is a much more empowering narrative, isn't it?

THE POWER OF GRATITUDE TO TRAIN ATTENTION

Keep in mind that gratitude trains us to use our attention in a very deliberate and specific way. For example, you can focus on what is wrong or missing in your life, and endlessly compare yourself to others. *Or,* you can intentionally turn your awareness toward noticing the good, decent, and beautiful things around you in this moment.

Why does this matter?

Life offers a full menu of items to choose from, and by choosing to notice what you could be grateful for, you cultivate a broader and more uplifting attitude about your situation. Gratitude is a selective attention practice that changes not only how you think and behave in the moment, but helps to develop a supportive and life-affirming habit for the future.

GRATITUDE ENCOURAGES HERE AND NOW PARTICIPATION

Gratitude is a proactive means of engaging in the here and now. We spend a lot of time as spectators—such as watching things on our computer, watching sports and entertainment on TV, and so on. With gratitude, however, you get in the game!

Using gratitude is like using your remote to turn on the present moment participation channel.

For example, in order to feel gratitude, you need to be present. You are encouraged to act on your gratitude because you feel more connected and optimistic as a result. Gratitude also helps build resilience because it gets us looking at the positives, rather than focusing on what's gone wrong.

EXERCISE: STARTING A DAILY GRATITUDE PRACTICE

Here are some simple practices for getting started with gratitude. The next time you notice negativity, use the jujitsu gratitude interventions below to turn negativity on its head.

Gratitude Practice #1: Notice and name one gratitude right now. Write this down, being sure to include *why* you are grateful or thankful. For example, this might look like: "I am grateful for ____ *because* ____." Telling why you are grateful adds richness to the story. Share your story with another, and learn about how the other person finds gratitude. Again, make sure to deepen the story by explaining *why* you are grateful.

Gratitude Practice #2: Keep track of your daily gratitude experiences. Get a teacup and tape the word "gratitude" on it. For each gratitude you find each day, put a penny in that cup, or write down on a small piece of paper two or three words about that gratitude. At the end of the week, review how many different ways you found and experienced gratitude.

Gratitude Practice #3: Share one daily gratitude with another. This is a wonderful way to make connections on a deeper level with others. Don't underestimate the importance of this for strengthening relationships, at home or the workplace.

Reflect on these questions:

- *How do you think gratitude could have a place in your life?*

- *What do you find the easiest part of noticing gratitude?*
  What is most difficult about the practice and why?

WHAT'S NEXT:

Practice using gratitude for a week and keep track of your attitude. Gratitude is just one type of attitude change that you can use to shift your day. Most importantly for the daily practice of mindfulness, feeling gratitude and expressing it helps us to transcend many of the hedonistic behaviors that arise to distract us. When we focus on the good we already have in our lives, we have less free attention for fixations on those negative pleasure-seeking pursuits.

MINDFUL SELF-CARE STEP 2 – RELATIONSHIPS

Everyone needs a sense of belonging. It's through relationships that we learn to grow. Sharing stories deepens our understanding of life and helps us learn new coping skills from others. Relationships are the life-blood for utilizing resources, gaining resilience and finding hope.

While much of the brain's social neural growth happens in the first 10-24 months of life through interactions with our caregivers, it continues as we grow older. While connecting with friends and others digitally can certainly be helpful—like when family and friends live out of town—keep in mind that your brain's social wiring and neural growth is accelerated when you are with someone in person, face-to-face.

For this reason, we need to continue to find safe and caring relationships so we can reach our maximum potential in developing relationships that support us at any age. But that's only part of the story, because scientists are now understanding how relationships can affect our health.

Could nurturing relationships lead to better health outcomes and greater longevity? To better understand this, researchers examined almost 150 studies in a meta-analytic review that included over 300,000 participants. They looked for factors that identified "a 50% increased likelihood of survival for participants with stronger social relationships." The study's results clearly showed that not having a supportive social network was as much a mortality risk as behaviors such as smoking cigarettes, alcoholism, and obesity.[4]

This may seem surprising, if not shocking, at first glance. But when you think about relationships as a buffer against stress and the vagaries of life, the importance of the quality of our relationships comes into focus.

Without question, those who populate your world have an effect on your mood and attitude. Even the choices you make with regards to listening to news and media can have a priming effect on how you feel. I'm not suggesting that you jettison associations that are not 100% positive ones, but to be more aware of whether or not your current relationships—and media usage (another kind of relationship)—is giving you what you need to nurture your growth and mindfulness. One suggestion later in this book is to find friends who are pursuing a mindfulness practice. In that way you will find like-minded persons with whom you can share your experiences. Let's explore this further right now.

EXPERIENCE: PLANTING A FRIENDSHIP GARDEN

Just as you can plant a garden in your backyard, you can plant seeds of friendship in your life. No matter how alone you may feel, the seeds you plant today will give you warmth and sustenance. Friends can transform life into something inspiring, uplifting and meaningful.

For 5-minutes, assess your existing friendship garden:

Reflect on these questions:

- *How many friends do you currently have in your garden? These are people who will really show up when you need support or a true face-to-face connection.*

- *How many minutes a day do you spend face-to-face with a significant someone in your life? Or, if it's not a significant person in your life, how much time do you spend interacting or sharing experiences with others face-to-face?*

- *How could you develop more opportunities to connect?*

- *How can you nurture existing friends or expand your garden, such as through the following?*

    —*Church or spiritual centers*
    —*Book and reading clubs*
    —*Hiking and sightseeing groups*
    —*Hobby clubs*
    —*Mindfulness, Meditation, Yoga, Tai Chi, etc.*

WHAT'S NEXT:
Here are three tips for increasing your friendship garden.

1) *Seize initiative.* This means that when you find a potential friend—or an existing one—take the initiative to ask them to meet with you.

2) *Have patience and take an interest.* Friendships take time to develop and deepen, but you can start by asking questions and taking an interest. Eventually, you can learn about an individual's history, likes, dislikes, interests, and more.

3) *Share your life and laughter.* Trust grows when you willingly share your life and experiences with your friends. Sharing humorous stories with your friends is a wonderful way to cultivate your friendship garden.

MINDFUL SELF-CARE STEP 3 – EATING & SLEEPING

Proper food and sleep are vital if you want to attain the levels of mental clarity necessary for mindfulness. Lacking either of these is like having a series of dominoes fall, because eating and sleeping are prerequisites for obtaining optimal cognitive functioning, concentration and emotional regulation. Here's the key thing to remember:

The thinking and executive center of the brain needs protein every two to three hours.

Protein matters because it breaks down into amino acids that are the building blocks for your neurotransmitters. Keep in mind that there are different kinds of neurotransmitters—some boost attention, some improve mood and mental flexibility, and others enhance memory and thinking. Lacking these neurotransmitters can have a dramatic effect on your ability to concentrate, think and behave.

One example of this was Yvonne, a 35-year old woman who was having trouble concentrating, was irritable with her family, and was emotionally upset much of the time. During our first session, I learned that Yvonne would skip breakfast and drink coffee until early afternoon when she had her first meal. After discovering that she had eaten peanut butter sandwiches in the past, Yvonne agreed to try an experiment for one week. She would eat a peanut butter sandwich in the morning and cut down on her coffee intake. When Yvonne came back the next week, she happily told me that her family noticed the difference in her mood and focus right away. I provided her with the food list below as a means of making sure she got enough protein.

This information includes very common foods—items that can be taken with you to use at work or during the day. This is not an exhaustive list, but it is a start to keeping your thinking brain online and functioning at its best.

FOODS FOR ATTENTION AND MOTIVATION

- Neurotransmitters **Norepinephrine** and **Dopamine**: synthesized from tyrosine; sources include almonds, lima beans, avocados, bananas, dairy, pumpkin and sesame seeds.

FOODS FOR CALM, MOOD REGULATION, AND THOUGHT FLEXIBILITY

- Neurotransmitter **Serotonin**: synthesized from tryptophan; sources include brown rice, cottage cheese, meat, turkey, peanuts and sesame seeds.

FOODS FOR THOUGHT AND MEMORY

- **Acetylcholine** (not made from amino acids): Choline

belongs to the B family of vitamins which is found in
lecithin. Foods include salmon, egg yolks, wheat
germ, soybeans, organ meats, and whole wheat
products.

It's also important to notice your patterns with regards to
alcohol and caffeine. If you currently have a problem with alcohol, you need to address this. One thing about mindfulness is
that it only works if we are honest with ourselves. Mindfulness
does not encourage us to hide from our habits, but to confront
whatever is happening in our life so that we can get free from
craving and addiction, as well as other unhealthy attachments
and desires.

As a highly caffeinated society, moderating coffee intake can
be a challenge. Interestingly, it was only 25 years after coffee
was introduced to England in the mid 17th century that King
Charles II banned coffee houses because of the fear that its
stimulating properties would foment political resistance. There
was such an uproar that the King rescinded his ban. I'm not
suggesting that anyone go cold turkey on java. However, it's
important to understand how caffeine affects the body and
mood so you can make your own informed decision. (In full
disclosure, I enjoy coffee, but watch my intake.)

Excess caffeine can impact mood and sleep. But how do we
measure this? One way is by examining how long caffeine stays
in the body. Caffeine has a very long half-life—that's amount of
time it takes for half of it to be metabolized by the liver and
removed from the body. Generally, caffeine remains in the
system for up to twenty-four hours or longer. This means that
for individuals who are sensitive to caffeine, a cup of coffee in
the afternoon might not only affect your sleep tonight, but
could also affect tomorrow's sleep. Of course, everyone has a
different sensitivity to caffeine. If you think caffeine is an issue,
cut down your use slowly. One gauge that lets you measure

your caffeine use is caffeine toxicity, which is about 1,500mg of caffeine daily.

To put that in perspective, a Starbucks Pike Place Venti (20 fluid ounces) contains 410mg of caffeine, while a Grande coffee (16 fluid ounces) contains 310mg of caffeine. That means that just four Venti-sized cups or five Grande-sized cups over a short time period could produce toxicity which could result in heartbeat irregularities, irritability, nausea and other symptoms. Most drip coffees are not that strong, but if you're not sure, you could use a website like *caffeineinformer.com* to check on the amounts of caffeine in products ranging from energy drinks and teas to coffee products.

SLEEP THE ULTIMATE HEALER

Sleep is vital for the care and well-being of your brain and body. New research has identified a system by which waste products are cleansed from the brain. It is called the glymphatic system, and according to Maiken Nedergaard, M.D., D.M.Sc., co-director of the Center for Translational Neuromedicine at the University of Rochester Medical Center (URMC) and lead author of the study, "Sleep is critical to the function of the brain's waste removal system and this study shows that the deeper the sleep the better. These findings also add to the increasingly clear evidence that quality of sleep or sleep deprivation can predict the onset of Alzheimer's and dementia."[5]

The glymphatic system only works when we sleep. Basically, it operates by compressing brain cells and pumping cerebral spinal fluid into the brain. This fluid cleanses out waste products, including the protein beta amyloid which is implicated in Alzheimer's.

If that doesn't convince you to guard your sleep, other studies show that lack of sleep can cause problems with everything from memory and processing emotions to learning and diabetes.

CREATING A SLEEP RITUAL FOR REST AND REJUVENATION

Consider developing your own sleep ritual that you can use to prepare you for sleep. It might help, for example, to think of your bedroom as a sacred sanctuary for rest and rejuvenation. One of the best ways to get a deeper sleep is by keeping the bedroom dark. Darkness signals your body to release the sleep hormone melatonin, which sets your sleep clock. However, if there is light coming in from outside or from another room, then your body's sleep clock could be delayed. Even the light from an LED clock can go through the eyelids and disrupt your sleep.

Now, let's consider how you could create a nighttime ritual that lets you prepare for sleep about an hour before bedtime. Here are some suggestions of activities you can do before entering your "sleep sanctuary":

- Avoid electroluminescence, such as light from the TV, computer, cell phone, etc.—all of which can delay your body's production of melatonin for up to two hours. If you have a TV or other media in your bedroom, start thinking about how you can create a tech free zone for sleep.
- Try drinking warm milk or chamomile tea at bedtime, which has known relaxation properties.
- Listen to calming or soothing music.
- Use a calming scent, such as lavender oil or rose oil.
- Read something that is not mentally stimulating or frightening. Reading in bed may actually keep you awake longer. So, save the reading for before you go to bed.

- Slip into comfortable sleepwear, a signal that you are preparing for sleep.
- Avoid exercise or eating at least an hour before bedtime, because these activities stimulate the body.

Even if you have an existing sleep habit, your body will change and adopt to the new program if you give it enough time and are consistent. Do your best to sleep at the same time each day, and eventually you will train your body and brain to follow along.

If you have trouble falling asleep, try the following relaxation meditation, which you can record and then play as needed. Or, you can practice it as often as needed until you feel comfortable and ready to use it at night.

EXPERIENCE: GUIDED SLEEP RELAXATION

This sleep relaxation practice consists of two parts. The first part will help release your body's muscular tension. The second part will relax your mind. You probably want to lie down, although you can do this while sitting down.

Before starting this exercise, take three deep breaths to prepare you for this sleep relaxation. Take one breath to release tension, one to release emotion, and one just for the fun of it. Take as long as you need to take those three calming breaths right now.

Part 1: Relaxing the Body

Practice for approximately 20 Seconds

For Step One, you will tense and relax the various parts of your body. For this process of tensing and relaxing, we'll start with your feet and slowly move up to your head and face. Have you ever done progressive muscle relaxation? This is a lot like that.

Start by tensing up your toes and soles of both feet for 10 seconds. Just count slowly to ten. Don't strain so hard that you hurt yourself. You're just tensing up so you can feel the muscles. If you feel the muscles growing tired and fatigued, that's okay. Try to keep them tense. You should be getting close to the count of ten by now.

When you reach ten, immediately let the toes and soles of your feet relax completely. Feel how different and relaxing it is to feel no tension in your feet. Spend the next 10 seconds or so focusing on what it feels like for your feet to be relaxed. If you want, you can even say to yourself something like, "All the tension in my feet is gone, my stress is slipping away and dissolving, I am really enjoying this feeling of deep relaxation and peace."

Practice for 20 seconds
As with any mindfulness practice, if your mind starts to wander, gently bring it back to each body group as you tense the muscles, then quickly release them. Right now, tighten your ankles on both legs. Count to ten as you feel all the muscles and tendons become stiff and tight. As you do this, keep all your other muscle groups—such as your legs and arms—relaxed. When you reach ten, let go. Feel how your ankles get soft, how the tension and stress are gone. Starting now, spend the next 10 seconds noticing the relaxation, and how the tissues deep in the ankle are free from any tension.

Practice for 20 seconds
Wonderful. Now, you'll move up to shins and calf of your lower legs. Tighten these muscles as you count to ten. They may grow tired and fatigued, but keep them as tense as you can. Now relax these muscles. Let them be free from any tension. Total relaxation and release. Pay attention to this for the next 10 seconds.

Practice for 20 seconds

Okay, now you're going to tense your leg muscles including your thighs and knees. Start counting to 10 as you feel all the muscles, even those you weren't aware of before. Let them contract as they tense up. They may grow tired and fatigued, but keep them as tense as you can. Keep going until you reach the count of ten, then let them go. Total relaxation, total freedom from tension, these legs that work so hard to support you during the day are now at peace, relieved of their hard work and given permission to rest... deep down into the knee and leg muscles. Spend a few more seconds to enjoy this feeling of relaxation.

Practice for 20 seconds

Next, moving up the body, tense the buttocks and pelvic region as you count to ten. Tighten this area as much as you can, holding it without straining too much. Feel how much tension there is, how many muscles there are. This even includes the tension that exists in your skeleton. See if you can feel it all. Good. Now, when you reach ten seconds, relax totally, completely. For the next 10 seconds, notice how this part of your body feels as you relax the muscles. Let any remaining tension or tightness drain out of you until this part of your body is at peace and calm. Enjoy this sensation of being free from tension.

Practice for 20 seconds

Now, for ten seconds, tense your abdomen and the muscles behind it in your lower back. Let this whole section tighten, even tightening the muscles at the side of your abdomen. Notice how this makes it hard for you to breathe. Stay with it for a few more seconds. Now, let this tightness release completely. How nice it is to breathe freely, to have your muscles in your lower back, even your spine, free from tension. Let yourself enjoy your body like this for a few more seconds as it lets go of this rigidity and becomes loose and peaceful.

Practice for 20 seconds
Moving up the body, tense your chest and upper back muscles as you count to ten. Hold them tightly, tightly, feeling how constricted they can be. As you do this, continue to breathe into your belly. Feel the tightness even in your rib cage and back, how your shoulder blades feel tense. Keep doing this for a few more seconds. Now let it go. Feel how quickly the tension lets go. Release it from your body and feel how so much of your body, from your toes to your chest, is now relaxed and calm. Enjoy this feeling for a few more seconds.

Practice for 20 seconds
Now, you're going to tighten your fists hard for ten seconds. Feel how the tightness extends into your fingers and into your wrists. This is what it is like to fight with daily tensions, all clenched up and nervous and strained. Does this feel familiar to you? Keep counting until you reach ten. Spend the next ten seconds releasing and letting your fingers, knuckles, and wrists relax and open. Can you feel the blood flow back in? Notice how nice it is not to live feeling clenched and straining. Feel the tension as it leaves each finger. Imagine letting it out like steam from a teapot. See the energy leaving like trails of steam rising from each fingertip… until there is no strain, no tension or clenching left.

Practice for 20 seconds
We're going to move up the arms. So, go ahead and tighten your biceps and elbows together, feeling all the muscles grow larger and tighter. As you do this, your hands hang, still completely relaxed. Keep feeling all the tension and fatigue in your biceps and elbows. Continue for a few more seconds. Now, let your

arms fall at your side, and feel the difference when you let the energy go. Just experience the looseness and flexibility in your arms for a few more moments.

Practice for 20 seconds
Slowly straighten your arms out, and for 10 seconds you'll tighten the triceps, the muscle on the back of your arm that opposes the biceps. Again, feel what it is like to clench and become rigid with this body group as you count. Feel the fatigue, the extension of the muscle into your arm for a few more moments. When you relax, let your arm fall, feeling the joy of letting go of this tension. There is no need to hold on to the tension, and your muscles want to relax.

Practice for 20 seconds
Next, tighten your neck and upper shoulders without straining. Feel how they carry so much tension. Hold this until you reach the count of ten. Relax immediately, letting your neck muscles and shoulders surrender to the feeling and peace that remains after the tightness is gone. Relax them even more deeply, letting your neck and shoulders sink more deeply into the floor or bed or wherever you are lying down.

Practice for 20 seconds
Your entire body is now relaxed with the exception of the face and skull. For ten seconds, you'll tighten this remaining part of the body. As you do this, imagine trying to make a fist with your face, tightening your eyes, scrunching up your cheeks, and at the same time, you feel your jaws open wider. Your lips are tight even though your mouth is open. Even feel your ears and scalp tighten and draw back. You didn't know you had so many muscles in your face, but now you feel them all, tight and fatigued.

Next, release all facial, scalp and skull tension as you picture your entire head and face growing smooth and long... your eyelids and eyebrows relaxing, your mouth and jaw letting go. All the skin on your face feels totally smooth and relaxed, with the sensation of deep tranquility, like it has had a gentle massage. Your ears and skull are free from any tension at all. Any remaining tension leaves your head and face, and now your whole body is relaxed, at rest, tension free. Spend a few extra moments enjoying this feeling. There is no need to be tense now, because this is your time to rest, and you can lead yourself through this body relaxation any time you want. And, if you want, you can alter the muscle relaxation to tighten and relax various parts of the face instead of the entire face at once. Feel free to alter the routine and find something that flows for you.

Part 2: Relaxing the Mind

After you complete this muscle relaxation, you can follow up by doing a mental relaxation practice for sleep. I suggest the use of a soothing word such as "calm, peace, relax, or love" to relax. You will mentally repeat the word as you take each in-breath and each out breath. This will block other racing thoughts, anxious thoughts, or worries that you may have, so that you can sleep. You can still use one of those words suggested earlier, or, you might try the word "sleep." Or you could say the word "rest" or even "restful sleep." If your mind wanders, just bring it back by simply noticing your breath as you set your intention to create and end each breath.

WHAT'S NEXT:
I hope this sleep relaxation is useful for you. Stick with it, and set your intention for a restful sleep before you even walk

in the bedroom. Feel free to alter this routine and find a combination that flows and works best for you.

MINDFUL SELF-CARE STEP 4 – ACTIVITY

Each of the steps to mindful self-care we've explored thus far produce a positive effect on both the brain and body, and activity is no different. Any moderate activity, such as walking briskly, stimulates a hormone in the brain known as brain-derived neurotrophic factor, or BDNF. Not surprisingly, BDNF has been called fertilizer for the brain because it stimulates neuronal growth and actually helps neurons make more connections with other neurons—essential ingredients for learning.

In his book *Spark: The Revolutionary Science of Exercise and the Brain*, John Ratey, MD, examines the fascinating story of how a revolutionary fitness program was implemented at a school district in Naperville, Illinois. Even in an admittedly economically disadvantaged school system, the fitness-based program was enough to boost resulting test scores on the Trends in International Mathematics and Science Study (TIMSS). On the science section of the study, Naperville's students scored first—as in first in the *world*. While this is just one example of how exercise supercharges the brain's ability to focus and learn, exercise stimulates a host of neurotransmitters and hormones that safeguard against anxiety, depression, ADHD, dementia, aging, and obesity.[6]

Don't make the mistake of thinking that an activity has to be going to the gym or running a marathon. You can do whatever activity you've enjoyed in the past that gets you moving, such as dancing, biking, swimming, or planting a garden. Don't forget walking the dog, since dogs make for excellent walking coaches!

Whatever the activity, consider adding the following components:

1) *Set a start date and time.* Schedule your activity as a way to maintain consistency.

2) *Start with small goals.* By starting small, you'll reach your goal and be bolstered by success. Over time you can increase the length and time of your activity.

3) *Find an activity buddy.* Having someone to walk or exercise with has a dual purpose. Firstly, a shared activity builds relationships and is more fun. Secondly, involving someone else adds the element of accountability. This can help you to stay motivated and engaged.

YOUR PORTABLE MINDFUL WALKING KIT

Did you ever stop to ask yourself how many hundreds if not thousands of steps you take every day? Since you're already walking, this could be the perfect opportunity for building a daily mindfulness practice.

Henry David Thoreau, the 19th century American author and philosopher, touched on this in his essay, *Walking*. He wrote, "But it sometimes happens that I cannot easily shake off the village. The thought of some work will run in my head, and I am not where my body is—I am out of my senses...What business have I in the woods, if I am thinking of something out of the woods?"[7]

The problem is that after learning to walk, we often do it automatically without really experiencing it deeply. After all, it gets us from one point to another. What else can it be good for, other than exercise and getting you somewhere?

When you are ready to stop mindlessly running around, you are ready for mindful walking.

Mindful walking is a way to invite new appreciation of the little things. It is portable. You can take it anywhere. You can use it anytime you choose. You can do it by yourself, or you can practice it with others. When integrated into your daily life, it becomes a seamless addition to your lifestyle, a way of being whose utter simplicity makes it a profoundly powerful tool for self-transformation. And yet, it's so easy to lose touch with the present moment and get distracted. Moving mindfully, you learn to walk and move in an entirely different way. However, you may not realize this if you are always moving quickly.

As an example, I once taught mindful walking to a group that included a woman who required a four-wheeled walker to keep her steady. She used the walker during our twenty-minute practice. Afterwards, when the group shared their experiences, the woman with the walker said, "I used to walk very fast, without paying attention. I had an accident because of that. If I had learned how to do mindful walking, I wouldn't be using this walker right now."

Mindful walking can be especially beneficial to neutralize the stress that often comes with major life changes, whether these transitions involve your work, relationships, or health challenges. It is a practice that keeps on giving.

EXPERIENCE: WALKING THE MINDFUL WALK

While doing this exercise, you may find that your mind gets distracted or goes elsewhere. This is normal. Just gently bring your mind and body back to the three steps—intention, action, and observation.

Experiment walking with and without shoes. Even a twenty or thirty-foot long space is enough for you to practice on. Once mindful walking feels more natural, you can use it to get present wherever you happen to be—outside or inside.

You will be using a three-step method that integrates mind and body in harmonious movement. It is really quite simple and elegant.

(1) *Intention.* Set an intention, which can be just taking a first step with one leg or the other.

(2) *Action.* Follow up the intention with an action...take that first step.

(3) *Observation.* Observe what happens, which means you take note of your physical movements along with any sensations or thoughts that arise.

The point is not to get robotic with walking, but to make the act of walking the object of your sustained attention. Do this, and you have turned the physical act into a mindful meditation.

If you find all of this to be awkward at first, remember those first baby steps you took before you learned to walk without effort. Mastery comes with practice. The more times you walk mindfully, the sooner this practice will become second nature for you.

Practice as follows for 3-Minutes

Standing, notice your feet on the floor. Don't worry about trying to take a breath with each step. Just let your breath be normal and rhythmic. You're going to start with a simple, single intention for each step.

Right now, set the intention to take a step with the right foot. Notice the movement of your leg, hip, and foot. Feel and observe your foot as it touches the ground. Next, set the intention to step with the left foot. Take several steps like this— mentally stating the intention to step with the right leg and then left leg.

Continue to walk like this for the next three-minutes. As you move, you can even set an intention for turning by mentally stating "turning, turning."

If you feel wobbly or unstable, you can speed up or stand near a wall to help support yourself. As you move about, allow your senses to expand all around, so you can notice even the little things in each micro-environment that you move through.

WHAT'S NEXT:

Admittedly, using multiple intentions can slow you down to the point where people might think you've become zombie-like. Fortunately, you can always practice mindfulness for a few minutes here and there in private. You can also use what I like to call real-time and real-speed mindfulness—which means being mindful even with normal movements.

You might try this by walking at a normal or brisk pace without multi-tasking by staying with the primary intention of "walking, walking, walking." Notice and observe all your movements as you move. Let your repeated intention keep you centered on the actions of your body. Whatever mindful self-care activity you use, you can bring full awareness to it.

MINDFUL SELF-CARE STEP 5 – TUNE-UP WITH MINDFULNESS

This last mindful self-care category is about paying attention to what you are *already* doing. You don't need to worry about the stress of adding anything on. Here are a few ideas that can bring structure to your daily mindfulness practice. If you decide to use any of these, write down what you'd like to practice and refer to it each day as a reminder.

1) *Once a day, eat one meal or one snack mindfully.* It's okay to start small. Even if you do this for just a few bites of a meal, you will bring mindful awareness to an action that is usually habituated. You can make any meal or morsel a meditation. In fact, research has shown that a mindful eating intervention for stress was helpful in reducing cortisol and abdominal fat in obese women.[8] Mindful eating gives individuals a greater sense of

control over food and greater comfort around food and body image.

There are a lot of books about mindful eating, from my own *12-Weeks to Mindful Eating Program*, *Art of the Inner Meal* and *Meal by Meal* to *Mindful Eating* by Jan Chozen Bays and *The Joy of Half a Cookie* by Jean Kristeller. The secret with eating mindfully is to know your hunger level and slow down to really taste the food. If your hunger is in an extreme range, it will be hard to make the right food choices regarding both the quantity and the type of food your body really needs. Mindful eating lets you be more purposeful about your food selection—even how many times you chew the food before swallowing.

I encourage a mindful eating practice because we eat thousands of meals in a lifetime. This offers a powerful means of practicing mindfulness while also promoting good health.

2) *Pick at least one daily activity to practice mindfully.* This could be anything. Whether it is taking a shower, walking your dog, washing dishes, whatever you choose, do it slowly enough and mindfully enough so that you are aware of all of your thoughts, feelings, movements and sensations.

3) *Treat your "ordinary" life moments with greater focus and attention.* Be mindfully aware of the details of what happens around you as you drive, work, garden, interact with strangers, or just observe the daily sunsets. This is one way to optimize and savor those otherwise "ordinary" moments.

If we really pay attention, most of us will find that we have more time on our hands than we may have imagined. What do you do when you are waiting in a line, for instance? Do you fantasize about the past or future? Do you dwell on your anxieties?

Why not begin by paying attention to the people who are in line with you? Pay attention to every detail of who they are and do so with mindful compassion for them. Get curious and pay attention to what you have never noticed before in your surroundings by finding something unique or pleasant.

Bringing Daily Practices All Together

This chapter offered a lot of practices and suggestions for cultivating mindfulness each day, especially with self-care. Keep track of how you are using these, and you may be surprised at the difference this makes in a short period of time. You can also decide to use daily mindfulness in a targeted way to help you find greater balance. Mindfulness teacher and Harvard Medical School psychology professor Ronald D. Siegel suggests various ways of using mindfulness as a sort of life preserver when the physical sensations of daily anxiety feel most apparent and potentially overwhelming. For example, he recommends a walking meditation if you are feeling particularly agitated or restless, since movement tends to reduce muscle tensions.[9] This offers more of an outer focus than the inner focus of a sitting meditation. Similarly, you could think about how to apply gratitude or any of the Five Steps to G-R-E-A-T Mindful Self-Care in order to counter challenges as you invite balance and well-being.

Use the experience below to help you reflect on these self-care strategies, and how you might start adapting them and integrating them into your life.

EXPERIENCE: STARTING DAILY SELF-CARE

Take a moment to reflect upon and answer these questions:

- *Which of the Five Steps to G-R-E-A-T Mindful Self-Care are you already finding natural and supportive?*

- *Of the G-R-E-A-T self-care strategies, which one(s) would you most benefit from by introducing it into your day?*

- *What practice would be most challenging to you? How could you start small and build success with this daily practice?*

- *How can you continue to move forward with your daily self-care—even when you feel tired, frustrated or impatient?*

WHAT'S NEXT:

As you start practicing—whether it's mindful self-care or another mindfulness practice, always remember that you can only eat an apple one bite at a time! In other words, go about your mindfulness practice with a sense of ease and grace. Invite inner hospitality and kindness as you undergo this work.

Just by noticing when you're not paying attention is a good mindfulness practice. Then, naturally come back to the moment, the precious here and now with one nice breath. How easy that is. How organic and natural.

In other words, just start where you are, with fresh awareness opening to the moment. There's nothing more or less to do.

How refreshing!

Key Chapter References

1. Emmons, R., McCullough, M. (2003) Highlights from the Research Project on Gratitude and Thankfulness. *http://local. psy.miami.edu/faculty/mmccullough/Gratitude-Related%20Stuff/ highlights_fall_2003.pdf* (accessed Nov. 1, 2019).

2. Lyubomirsky, Sonja. (2008) *The How of Happiness: A New Approach to Getting the Life You Want.* New York: Penguin.

3. Bartlett, M.Y., DeSteno D. (2006) Gratitude and prosocial behavior: helping when it costs you. *Psychological Science.* 2006 Apr; 17(4):319-25.

4. Holt-Lunstad, Smith, and Layton, Social Relationships and Mortality Risk: A Meta-analytic Review. *PLOS Medicine,* July 27, 2010 https://doi.org/10.1371/journal.pmed.1000316.

5. University of Rochester Medical Center. (2019, February 27). Not all sleep is equal when it comes to cleaning the brain. *ScienceDaily.* Retrieved November 1, 2019 from www. sciencedaily.com/releases/2019/02/190227173111.htm.

6. Ratey, John. (2013) *Spark: The Revolutionary New Science of Exercise and the Brain.* New York: Little, Brown and Company.

7. Thoreau, Henry David. (2000) *Walden and Other Writings.* Boston: Adamant Media.

8. Jennifer Daubenmier, Jean Kristeller, Frederick M. Hecht, et. al., "Mindfulness Intervention for Stress Eating to Reduce Cortisol and Abdominal Fat among Overweight and Obese Women: An Exploratory Randomized Controlled Study," Journal of Obesity, vol. 2011, Article ID 651936, 13 pages, 2011. https://doi.org/10.1155/2011/651936.

9. Siegel, R.D. (2010) *The Mindfulness Solution.* New York: Guilford.

4

ENHANCE WORKING
ENVIRONMENTS WITH WELLNESS

*P*eople seem to either love their work life, merely tolerate it, or they flat out hate it. In this chapter, we're expanding the word work to include such things as a job that pays the bills, schooling for students, caregiving, parenting, and any other responsibilities or obligations that you may carry.

When we love our work, we feel 'in the flow' and the more we have this optimal experience, the better we feel about ourselves and our life. That translates into expressing more happiness. But even in this wonderful state of fulfillment, we must manage some degree of stress. If your job and the challenges it brings feel more like a nightmare than a joy, then stress can be a compounding problem that brings mental anguish, health problems, and interpersonal relationship issues.

Levels of stress influence on-the-job happiness, and it is this happiness—or the lack of it—that affects performance. This is an insight developed over the past decade by economists and psychologists who have come to realize that emotions in business and the workplace matter more than most company executives would like to confess.

A survey conducted yearly by the American Psychological

Association over the past 10 years has consistently shown that Americans are highly stressed. Some of these APA surveys indicated that as many as seventy-seven percent of adults experienced physical symptoms in the previous month from stress, including fatigue, headaches, upset stomach, muscle tension, teeth grinding, lack of appetite, insomnia, and changes in sex drive. Seventy-three percent reported psychological symptoms from stress such as irritability, anger, sadness and tearfulness. Forty-three percent either ate unhealthy foods or ate excessively in response to the job stress.[1] The 2019 survey showed that six in every 10 adults cited work and money as major stressors, with increased worries about terrorism, the election, and the cost of health care, to name a few.[2] What we worry about may change over time, but overall stress may actually rise because of new and immediate concerns.

How does happiness or unhappiness affect job performance? Another revealing survey, this one done by *The Gallup Management Journal* and the Gallup polling organization, questioned about 1,000 employed adults to determine how happiness and well-being affected their job performance. Three types of employees were identified: 1) 27% of those surveyed were engaged, feeling a connection to their job and company, and working with passion. 2) 59% of respondents were not-engaged and had 'checked out,' spending their time sleepwalking through each workday. 3) 14% were actively disengaged, busy acting out their unhappiness by undermining productivity.[3]

"Negative feelings at work also seem to spill over into actively disengaged workers' home lives," commented the Gallup researchers. "The survey asked respondents if they had three or more days in the past month when work stress caused them to behave poorly with friends or family members. More than half (54%) of actively disengaged workers and 31% of not-engaged workers answered yes to this question, while just 17%

of engaged workers answered yes. These results are similar to those reported in previous surveys."

Once the Gallup findings are extrapolated out to the U.S. workforce as a whole, this means that about 19.2 million workers in this country are actively disengaged from their jobs. The estimated cost to the U.S. economy, as calculated by the Gallup Organization, may be at least $300 billion a year in lost productivity.

Yet, despite this level of disengagement, Gallup researchers also reported, "happy and engaged employees are much more likely to have a positive relationship with their boss, are better equipped to handle new challenges and changes, feel they are more valued by their employers, handle stress more effectively, and are much more satisfied with their lives."[4]

The question, then, is this: How can we evolve our workplace environments so that they produce relationships that are nourishing, satisfying and positive? Before exploring this further, let's take a moment to explore your own relationship with your work—again, we're taking the broader view of work to include being a student, employee, parent and so on.

EXPERIENCE: REFLECTION ON WORKPLACE STRESS

Take a moment to reflect upon and answer these questions:

- *How would you rate your level satisfaction and happiness with the kind of work that you're doing?*

- *What are the greatest sources of stress in your work? How do these affect job satisfaction and performance? How do these affect your health?*

- *How could you integrate a short (7-15 minute) mindful breathing practice, or any other awareness behavior into your day as a way to shift your workplace experience?*

WHAT'S NEXT:

As you go through your work day, begin noticing opportunities for developing presence as you savor the here and now. Create a plan for using a meditative practice daily and keep track of how that makes you feel, as well as how others respond to you.

THE MINDFUL ANTIDOTE TO WORKPLACE STRESS

The good news is that your working environment tells only part of the story. It's the level of mindfulness you bring to the workplace that has the power to truly transform your day to day experience. According to a study published in *Organizational Behavior and Human Decision Processes*, the answer to creating a nurturing workplace could be using a simple mindfulness practice. The study's subjects, who worked for an insurance company, practiced a short, focused breathing meditation for only 7-15 minutes. This brief practice produced the following results:

- Pro-social behavior towards customers and colleagues. In other words, those doing the mindfulness practice were more giving of their time and showed a greater desire to help others.
- Financial generosity toward others. It wasn't just time that the mindfulness practitioners were willing to

extend to others. Being financially generous was another measure of giving and altruism.

- Increased empathy, compassion, and a willingness to understand the perspectives of other persons. Both a focused breathing meditation and the loving-kindness practice were shown to produce these emotional components of openness.

Researchers concluded, "Our results indicate that secular state mindfulness can make people more other-oriented and helpful. This benefit holds even in the workplace, where being helpful toward others might face constraints but is nevertheless of great importance."[5]

All this was possible with a modest investment of just seven minutes of time. Contrast this with the mindlessness that exacerbates stress, fatigue, and burnout in any work environment. Burnout can be viewed as a culture of overwork where self-care is neglected. This is why the *Five Steps to G-R-E-A-T Mindful Self-Care* from Chapter 3 are effective tools.

For some work settings—hospitals and emergency rooms, for example—little mindless errors in judgment endanger lives. It's no wonder that some workplaces post large signs saying simply, *PAY ATTENTION.* But why use a fear-based warning when you can use a method that organically grows presence that is steeped in generosity, empathy and care for others?

Certainly, there are some common-sense approaches that anyone can take to make the workplace more livable. For example, Richard O'Connor, author of *Undoing Perpetual Stress*, recommends that whenever possible, "employees have to take the initiative to apply mindfulness principles at work: by taking frequent stretch breaks, walking at lunch, avoiding caffeine in favor of herbal teas. Bring in a book of meditations and read a page every hour or so. Decorate the cubicle...have pictures of loved ones...have a plant..."[6] These are all helpful ideas, and they can easily be adapted to educational and other environments. But let's look at a more systematic approach for profoundly altering the workplace by applying mindfulness.

Research from the fields of psychology and business administration has uncovered five key ways that mindfulness practices can play positive roles in any work-related environment:

1) Mindfulness helps create order

2) Mindfulness overcomes fixed mindsets and sharpens creativity

3) Mindfulness widens external attention

4) Mindfulness reduces negativity and stress

5) Mindfulness addresses communication problems

Each of these areas provides a hopeful and fresh point of view for how to integrate mindfulness into the workplace. Let's investigate each of these more closely.

1—MINDFULNESS CREATES ORDER

Here is how Michael Carroll, a veteran of 20 years in corporate America, in his book, *Awake at Work: 35 Practical Buddhist Principles for Discovering Clarity and Balance in the Midst of Work's Chaos*, describes the chaotic condition of many work environments: "Work will not stay in place, despite all our efforts. Financial reports and spreadsheets bring the appearance of order. Routines and schedules seem reliable. Our computer systems and management abilities offer a certain kind of predictability. But what we set out wanting to do at work is never what we end up with. Work, by its nature, is unpredictable and messy, chaotic and surprising."[7]

Because we can never have a completely neat and tidy relationship with our career, Carroll urges us to develop a mindful attitude of acceptance that work can be a mess because of its very nature (as is all of life), and we should relax, not try to control too much, and allow ourselves to be curious about the surprises that our livelihoods bring to us.

Mindfulness practice can provide us with both the overview and neutral perspective necessary to view this messiness with acceptance and humor. This gives us the opportunity to make our work part of the very core of our spiritual lives.

Ironically, when we release the need to micromanage and constantly control, an amazing thing often happens—order tends to emerge from seeming chaos. It starts with the order that is established within our minds from mindful engagement with our tasks. As more of our colleagues act mindfully on the job, a synergy of orderliness is given an opportunity to smooth the appearance and feeling of disorder.

EXPERIENCE: REFLECTION ON WHAT YOU CAN'T CONTROL

Take a moment to reflect upon and answer the following:

- *Make note of everything that you can't control in your workplace. This could be deadlines, other's moods, unproductive co-workers, review procedures, the time clock, etc.*

- *What would it be like to cultivate an attitude of acceptance toward the chaos or out of control situations in your workplace? What would you gain by doing so?*

• *How could you bring order to what you can control—such your own office, desk, or workspace?*

WHAT'S NEXT:

Acceptance is an empowering tool for overcoming those "impossible" things that you can't control. Keep in mind that acceptance is not submission or giving up. Rather, it's a recognition that you have a real choice about how to respond to the disorder or chaos. As time goes on, increase your level of acceptance, and see how this allows you to move more easily through your day. Acceptance is like being on a sturdy boat that stays afloat regardless of the ebb and flow of the waves.

2—MINDFULNESS OVERCOMES FIXED MINDSETS

Practically all of the advantages of mindfulness can be found and used in the workplace, says Harvard psychologist and researcher Ellen J. Langer. According to Langer, mindful supervisors and employees are the ones who notice the early warning signs of job problems "before they become serious and dangerously costly. Whether it is a slight shift on a dial in a nuclear energy plant, or the first hint of what Theodore Levitt of the Harvard Business School calls the 'shadow of obsolescence,' the early signs of change are warnings and, to the mindful, opportunities."[8]

One of the hallmarks of mindlessness is being stuck in a fixed mindset—which means you are unable to be adaptable and creative. Fixed mindsets are pre-determined cognitive beliefs. One example of an unwillingness to see things differently is typified by the worn phrase, "we've always done things this way."

In one study Langer conducted, a woman pretended to have

sprained her knee, just outside a pharmacy. When passers-by stopped to help, the woman asked if that person could go into the pharmacy and get her an Ace Bandage. The pharmacy, which was in on the study, had removed all the Ace Bandage branded items. There were still bandages, but no Ace Bandages. Most people came out of the store empty-handed because they were fixed on the pre-cognitive mindset of thinking that only an Ace Bandage would do the job.

Fixed mindsets can cause conflict, fatigue and burnout. Another form of fixed mindset is a belief in limits, which is a creativity killer that produces conformity and stifles innovation, flexibility and productivity. A belief in limits can make it hard to find novel ways to approach almost anything. One famous example of a fixed limit long held to be true was that "it's physically impossible for a human being to run the mile in under 4-minutes" (a widely held belief until Roger Bannister did otherwise).

Context is another important element that can keep creativity from being applied. A shift in context regarding how we perceive our work, for example, can completely change how we feel and act. Reexamining the type of role one plays in terms of how a job benefits society—and not just that individual and the company—could facilitate the ability of workers to change responsibilities within a business structure, or even to switch careers if need be. When you alter your perspective about the context within which you perform your job, you can go from being bored to being excited, creative, and passionate about the work you do every day.

Entrepreneurs and students, for example, will find a mindfulness practice especially useful in honing both communication skills and sensing the need for innovative solutions to problems. Applying a mindful quality of openness and flexibility to problem solving—"meditating on it" and "letting it go" instead of forcing an answer—shifts the context within which you view the challenge. Instead of creating stress, this shift of always seeing a problem as an opportunity forges a mindset of passion and enthusiasm. The objective observer within you cultivated by mindfulness senses new direction, interconnections, and synergies that a rigid and reactive mind overlooks.

During a sabbatical at the Harvard Business School, Professor Langer and her colleagues came up with these slogans that should be plaques on the desk of every entrepreneur and business manager:

Mindlessness is the application of yesterday's business solutions to today's problems.

Mindfulness is attunement to today's demands to avoid tomorrow's difficulties.[9]

EXPERIENCE: MINDFUL UMBRELLA TECHNIQUE

This is a simple and fun way to find new answers when stuck. There are three steps to this technique. (Note: This umbrella technique was used by writers on one of TV's earliest variety comedy sketch programs, *Your Show of Shows*.)

1) Think of a career choice or work-related problem (or any problem) that you are facing. Write that down as a question, such as "What kind of job would I love to do most?"

2) Draw the shape of an umbrella on a sheet of paper, or use the space provided on the next page.

3) In the space beneath the curved umbrella, write down ALL of the ideas that come to mind relating to the topic or idea that you want to explore.

Let your mind flow. Do this without censoring anything. Let every idea that emerges be acceptable to go under your umbrella. Don't judge it. In this way, you can overcome obstacles such as a belief in limits, fixed mindsets and contexts.

Give yourself permission to be creative and free and even silly with your thoughts. In this way you can harness the creative insights of the right hemisphere of your brain.

This mindfulness brainstorming exercise in creativity can be performed by yourself, or with a group. Experiment with what emerges, and see what best fits the circumstances.

WHAT'S NEXT:

Your open and flexible thinking is like a superpower that can help you adapt in novel ways to the situations and problems you face. A good way to start is by simply noticing those fixed mindsets—and don't worry, because we all have them. An awareness of fixed mindsets is the first step to releasing them. Before long, you might even find yourself asking, "why does it have to be done like this?"

3—MINDFULNESS WIDENS EXTERNAL ATTENTION

How managers and employees focus their attention in corporate structures has become a growing field of research in business graduate schools, and the effects of mindfulness on how individuals perform their work tasks is seen as a key function. The term used for mindfulness applied to dynamic task environments (where decisions occur rapidly and are interconnected) is a 'wide external breadth of attention.'

Because innersight awareness, as described in Chapter 2, trains selective attention, it can also be used to broaden that awareness as needed. A Rice University professor in the Graduate School of Business, Erik Dane, studied the benefits of maintaining a wide external breadth of attention as used by trial lawyers in Houston. "Because of the dynamic nature of trials," Dane wrote in the *Journal of Management*, "it is imperative for lawyers to gain as much information as possible from the courtroom environment to make effective decisions. Mindfulness was found to play a key role toward this end because it permits lawyers to attend to a wide range of phenomena, including the reactions of the judge, jury members, and opposing lawyers—critical inputs for making decisions about when and how to employ their arguments and other persuasive tactics."[10]

Within companies, this wide external attention form of mindfulness helps managers to improvise in the face of unexpected challenges, and to make interdependent decisions in real time, which is to say, "fight fires" and respond to crises. Successful improvisation in business depends on being attentive and alert to what is happening in the here and now.

EXPERIENCE: REFLECTION ON WIDENING ATTENTION

Take a moment to reflect upon these questions:

- *When in the past have you needed to expand your attention during a crisis? How well did that process help you maintain a sense of equanimity and calmness?*

- *How can your mindfulness practice help you expand*

awareness in a selective and beneficial way so that you respond without being reactive, rigid or confused?

WHAT'S NEXT:

Moving forward, get into the practice of tuning in to your body. This helps you to recognize when and where you get tight, constricted and defensive. For example, you might notice how the body responds to tension the next time you feel angry, upset or defensive. Where are you clenched up—in the arms, the jaw, the neck and shoulders, the hands? Allow these parts of the body to relax as you broaden out your attention and become more receptive. When connecting with others, bring mindful awareness to using body language that is open and non-threatening.

4—MINDFULNESS REDUCES NEGATIVITY AND STRESS

An article on mindfulness in work environments, published in the *Journal of Academic and Business Ethics,* concluded that mindfulness, if used by employees and managers, "can interrupt their self-defeating and irrational thoughts and {they can} become more focused on their job responsibilities. They will become better able to cope and manage the bombardment of information, accept change in a more realistic and healthy manner, and realize greater fulfillment in both their professional and personal lives."[11]

An added benefit is that "a reduction of stress will increase employee satisfaction and improve work enthusiasm and productivity." The author of this article identified three beliefs that are critical to the success of mindfulness in improving overall productivity: 1) accepting that life isn't fair; 2) learning to deal with the truth of any situation; and 3) knowing that one has the ability to choose one's attitude.

Each of these three ideas points out that it is easier to live in what I prefer to think of as 'the what is' as opposed to 'the what if.' The practice of mindfulness helps us face difficult situations directly. With mindfulness we don't need to try and escape, put our heads in the sand, or avoid unwanted circumstances. By recognizing and facing situations as they truly are, the amount of stress and negativity that anyone might ordinarily feel is reduced dramatically. Recognition means that we can take steps to manage that stress, use mindfulness and relaxation practices to buffer from it, or realize that the stressor is temporary and not permanent.

There is still another dimension of stress around work that involves compulsions or obsessions. Compulsions around work and career can manifest in several ways. Some people work compulsively and need a mindfulness practice to better balance their mind, their priorities, and their life. Other people avoid productive work in a compulsive way, either not working at all, or taking unchallenging jobs far below their capacity to achieve. Mindfulness can give them a chance to recognize and awaken to the hidden drivers behind work attitudes and behaviors—such as a fear of failure or feelings of low self-worth.

Whatever approach you take to your work, setting healthy boundaries is a powerful method for reducing negativity and stress. If you feel overwhelmed by work or feel that it consumes your life even when you come home, try the following experience.

EXPERIENCE: REFLECTION ON WORK BOUNDARIES

Take a moment to reflect upon these questions:

- *What are your current work boundaries? Do you feel*

overwhelmed by work? Does work follow you home (via calls, text, emails, deadlines, etc.).

- *How does work affect your relationships outside of the workplace?*

- *What one small mindful boundary change around work would bring more balance into your life? (Things such as: saying no to that extra project when you already can't finish your work, not bringing work home, and allowing time for hobbies and interpersonal relationships, etc.)*

WHAT'S NEXT:
Remember that you don't need to do everything all at once. Even small boundary changes, done over a period of time, can help reduce stress. These boundary changes can also relate to the boundaries you set at home with technology. Collapsing in front of the TV after a long day might let you zone out. But if that TV watching becomes a mindless habit, then you might be missing out on other, more nurturing and satisfying opportunities such as meaningfully connecting with others.

5—MINDFULNESS ADDRESSES COMMUNICATION PROBLEMS

In his book *Lead Your Boss: The Subtle Art of Managing Up*, internationally recognized leadership consultant John Baldoni writes, "Organizations must be filled with people who can think for themselves as well as act with initiative and make good things happen. Such behaviors allow each level of management to engage strategically as well as execute tactically."[12] Such an open flow of communication from middle management *up* to higher levels requires qualities like openness and trust. The challenge for business is how to create an atmosphere that facilitates these qualities.

Conflict management research has documented how dysfunctional communication sets in motion "relatively mindless cycles of blaming. During these cycles, each party focuses on the faults of the other, listens ineffectively to the partner, and overlooks his or her own contributions to the problem," according to a 2000 study in the *Journal of Social Issues.* "Competent conflict management tactics appear to be those that increase the mindfulness of conflict behavior."[13]

Beyond helping to prevent miscommunication and its role in resolving conflicts, mindful listening in a business environment can facilitate a more effective hiring and longer retention of employees. This occurs in three keys areas: 1) the job interview, where mindful listening can be important traits to cultivate and bestow advantages for both company interviewers and job applicants; 2) the expectations of new employees, where mindfulness training can help to prevent unrealistic expectations that lead to eventual dissatisfaction and negativity on the job; and 3) the area of performance feedback, where mindful feedback behavior by both supervisors and employees can help encourage both to reflect and relate in fresh and open ways, without succumbing to old conditioning or reactivity.

Ellen J. Langer and Mihnea Moldoveanu, writing in the *Journal of Social Issues,* make the point that "mindful communication is, to a large extent, about mindful listening: listening that is unencumbered by preexisting categories that constrain the attention of the listener to a pre-specified set of characteristics of the other." They advocate mindfulness programs in large institutional settings "to provide cognitive skills that keep alternative interpretations open even as we are busy responding on the basis of already-settled-on interpretations of another person's behavior."[14]

On-the-job mindfulness training provides a host of other opportunities to reduce miscommunication in the workplace and in so doing, ameliorates stress, negativity, and drains on productivity. Relationships between managers and employees can be improved through a mindful re-set with various stress reduction, attunement and mindfulness trainings. The same holds true for relations between workers with different cultural backgrounds.

EXPERIENCE: REFLECTION ON ADDRESSING COMMUNICATION

Reflect upon these questions:

- *What are the challenges you face in the workplace with regards to communication?*

- *How can a mindfulness practice help you 'lead' others in the workplace to reduce misunderstanding?*

WHAT'S NEXT:

Consider how you can broaden your perspective when discussing ideas with others. This way, you can bring openness and a sense of empathy that deepen any communication. In the next chapter, we'll touch upon listening and communication in more detail.

. . .

MINDFUL TRANSITION POINTS FOR WORK

People often experience anxiety when transitioning because the brain's survival center—the amygdala—is on high alert whenever there's uncertainty about what will happen next. Knowing how to identify transition points at work lets you integrate these as mindful moments. This doesn't demand any extra time or effort, but may reduce stress and make each day more fulfilling and memorable.

- **Going to Work**

For the reasons mentioned above, it is not uncommon for some to become anxious on the way to work. Fortunately, mindfulness is a key for staying present, not to be at work in your mind before you even get there. If driving, notice your hands on the steering wheel and your body in the seat. You might consider listening to music that is calming or uplifting.

Whatever your means of getting to work—driving, walking, biking, or taking public transportation—use mindfulness to keep you centered on the present moment. Notice pleasantness in your surroundings. Take a curious stance, such as trying a different route to work.

- **Starting Work**

You may want to create a small ritual that eases you into your workday—whether that is enjoying a cup of hot tea or coffee (beware of too much caffeine). How you greet others can make a difference to the connection you feel in the workplace. It's advisable to have a pleasant greeting with at least one person when you arrive. In addition, you might inwardly state an intention of what you hope to accomplish during the day or how your work will benefit others and yourself.

- **Break Time**

This can be a wonderful transition point for doing something nurturing. Even a short walk outside to look at the trees, the sky, or the grass can be soothing. You can practice an abbreviated version of the body scan (Chapter 5) or just do some breathing. This can also be a good time to journal gratitude—and help you come back to your job in a balanced and appreciative state of mind.

- **Meetings**

Anytime that we are faced with uncertainty can increase feelings of anxiety and stress. If meetings do this to you, consider practicing mindful walking on the way to the meeting. As described in Chapter 3, you can walk mindfully at normal pace and no-one will know that you are practicing being fully present, feeling each step and turn of the body as you walk.

During meetings, you can practice attunement skills and non-judgmental observation. Give yourself the freedom to share your thoughts with others in an authentic and kind way.

- **Lunch**

Many people eat lunch at work while mutli-tasking—working on the computer, answering e-mail, and generally diminishing the importance of food to being nothing more than fuel for the body and mind. According to food psychologist and researcher Brian Wansink, author of *Mindless Eating: Why We Eat More Than We Think*, "We overeat not because of hunger but because of family and friends, packages and plates, names and numbers, labels and lights, colors and candles, shapes and smells, distractions and distances, cupboards and containers…

Most of us are blissfully unaware of what influences how much we eat."[15]

Distraction is one major cause of not tasting food and eating too much food. Mindful eating is a process that changes that because it alters the very *relationship* you have with food. Give some thought to how you can give yourself the time to eat in a nourishing way at work.

- **Leaving**

You might want to think about reflecting on the day's accomplishments and connections that you made. For example, see if you can recall one moment of levity that you enjoyed with another. Let your trip back home be a time that you can start discharging and letting go of tension that has accumulated from the work domain. Consider, too, that the skills often demanded in the workplace—the need for control, efficiency, promptness, cleanliness, etc.—do not always translate to the home environment. To expect or require this would mean being trapped in the work context and not having the flexibility to shift to a new context.

EXPERIENCE: WORK TRANSITION POINTS

Reflect on the following questions:

- *Which work transition points are the easiest for you to handle? What are you doing that helps you transition?*

- *Which transitions are most stressful or difficult for you to manage?*

- *How could you bring mindfulness into even one challenging and stressful transition point?*

WHAT'S NEXT:

Start noticing how you feel as you are about to transition. Does it bring up worry, anxiety, or any other feeling? Pay attention to how you can settle down after making any transition. Remember, too, that it's normal to feel unsettled during times of transition—so invite self-kindness as you grow more aware of these moments and how to manage them.

To conclude this chapter, let's try a mindfulness practice that gets you very present using the body. This takes only a couple of minutes, and it's portable so you can use it anywhere, anytime. Mindfulness of the body is helpful because when we get grounded in the body, the mind quiets down and doesn't wander as much.

Note: Use this practice either before or after transitioning as a way to help you settle down and get focused and calm.

EXPERIENCE: PALM THE PRESENT MOMENT—A TRANSITION PRACTICE

*Find a quiet place where you can practice, either indoors or outside. In this simple practice, you will slowly touch your palms, but you'll do so in a very slow and deliberate way that lets you experience even the subtlest sensation. (**If you feel any pain because of a position or tension, feel free to release or shift that position to reduce pain.**)*

1) Begin sitting or standing. After settling in, rub your hands

briskly together for about five seconds. Next, raise your hands in front of your chest, with hands about one or two feet apart.

2) Slowly bring your hands together, pausing the moment you sense any heat, warmth, energy, or pressure. You might even imagine that energy as a ball or sphere between your hands. How heavy is it? What color?

3) Continue to slowly bring the hands closer together. You might notice that you have to press against a feeling of heat, energy or pressure. Continue until the fingertips lightly touch.

4) With the fingertips touching, slowly bring the hands closer until the palms touch. Notice how the fingers straighten and which parts of the hands make contact—*even before the palms come into contact.*

5) Raise your elbows up and press your palms together fairly hard for the count of five (less if you feel pain).

6) Lower the elbows and shoulders to let go of the tension.

7) Open your hands, and as you do, feel the sensation in the palms. Slowly let the arms come down to rest onto your legs.

8) Lastly, imagine breathing into the body where any tension, tightness, or negativity remains. Then as you exhale, you might picture the tension or tightness or negativity as it drains out down the legs and out the bottom of your feet and back into the Earth for recycling. Take as many of these harmonizing breaths as necessary until you feel calm and centered.

- *How did this practice feel for you? It's best to practice it more than once until you can do it by memory.*

- *When would be a good time for you to Palm the Present Moment? How could it help with even one daily transition?*

WHAT'S NEXT:

You just contacted the here and now in a powerful way. This brief mindfulness meditation is ideal for getting refreshed anytime you feel scattered, distracted, overwhelmed or in transition. For *Palm the Present Moment* to be effective, however, you need to practice is several times. You will soon find it to be an easy and all-natural way to get present and focused.

The next time you get very embodied—whether playing a sport, taking a nice, long breath or bringing your palms together—you might even ask the rhetorical question: *Is what I'm feeling right now 'yesterday'? Is it 'tomorrow'?* Of course, it's very much the present moment.

Key Chapter References

1. American Psychological Association (2007). *Stress in America.* http://www.APApractice.org.

2. American Psychological Association (2019). *Stress in America.*

https://www.apa.org/news/press/releases/stress/?tab=1

3. Krueger, J, Killham, E. (2005) At Work, Feeling Good Matters. *Gallup Management Journal.* 2005 Dec 8; http://gmj.gallup.com.

4. Same as 3.

5. Andrew C. Hafenbrack, Lindsey D. Cameron, Gretchen M. Spreitzer, et. al., (2019) Helping People by Being in the Present: Mindfulness Increases Prosocial Behavior. *Organizational Behavior and Human Decision Processes.* https://doi.org/10.1016/j.obhdp.2019.08.005.

6. O'Connor, R. (2006) *Undoing Perpetual Stress.* New York: Berkley.

7. Carroll, M. (2004) *Awake at Work: 35 Practical Buddhist*

Principles for Discovering Clarity and Balance in the Midst of Work's Chaos. Boston: Shambhala.

8. Langer, E. J. (2014) *Mindfulness.* New York: Da Capo Press.

9. same as 8.

10. Dane, E. (2010) Paying Attention to Mindfulness and Its Effects on Task Performance in the Workplace. *Journal of Management.* 2010 April 9: http://doi:10.1177/0149206310367948.

11. Fries, M. (2008) Mindfulness Based Stress Reduction for the Changing Work Environment. *Journal of Academic and Business Ethics.* 2008 Vol. 2. http://citeseerx.ist.psu.edu/viewdoc/download?doi=10.1.1.512.3021&rep=rep1&type=pdf. Accessed Dec. 2019.

12. Baldoni, J. (2009) *Lead Your Boss: The Subtle Art of Managing Up.* New York: AMACOM.

13. Burgoon, J.K. et al. (2000) Mindfulness and Interpersonal Communication. *Journal of Social Issues.* 2000; 56(1): 105-127.

14. Langer, E.J., Moldoveanu, M. (2000) Mindfulness Research and the Future. *Journal of Social Issues.* 2000; 56(1):129-139.

15. Wansink, B. (2007) *Mindless Eating: Why We Eat More Than We Think.* New York: Bantam.

INVITE MINDFULNESS INTO HEART AND HOME

*W*hen you embody wholeness, clarity, love, and act with the utmost regard, respect and kindness for others, you touch the very heart of mindfulness. In this chapter, you'll find four key approaches designed to train your awareness and produce thinking and actions that are ethical and beneficial. These include 1) the practice of gratitude, 2) the body scan, 3) the loving-kindness meditation, and 4) the use of sacred space and rituals. Together, these will help you develop the habits of effort and discipline necessary to turn your life toward joy and happiness.

While you can apply these four practices anywhere, they play an essential role in establishing a flourishing and peaceful home environment. These put an emphasis on slowing down, taking your time, and appreciating the little things. This style of living, however, is often at odds with the focus on material goods rather than relationships.

This may be especially true in the U.S., where the average shopper is over stimulated in every way possible, from TV shopping networks and giant superstores to tempting pop-up offerings on smart phones—where your fingertip hovers one precarious click away from ordering almost everything imaginable. It's a retailer's dream.

Back in the 1970s, two psychologists at Northwestern University, Philip Brickman and Donald Campbell developed the theory of the *hedonic treadmill* to account for compulsive urges of many shoppers and eaters. Their concept was founded on the basis that people are genetically wired, or driven, to seek out what is novel and pleasurable. If you're going to invite mindfulness, then you need to be aware of those things that block or obstruct it. Now, through brain science, we know that the brain releases dopamine in anticipation of a reward. This is a powerful impulse, and one that I've seen is strong enough to pull individuals into internet porn addiction.

Putting this into a retail context, it works because people get a positive feeling, or reward, from buying novel things—new food items, clothes, electronic gadgets, jewelry, etc. Regardless of how much pleasure is initially derived, however, our emotional systems require newness. Eventually, the allure of that new shiny item wears off, and soon we need more and more of the "consumption drug" to feel the same high feeling. Before long, we are on the hedonic treadmill, and things we never cared about before become things we now can't live without. With this as background, let's begin with gratitude, initially described as the first step to mindful self-care.

GRATITUDE PRACTICE: FINDING CONNECTION

Since gratitude is such a useful antidote to the hedonic treadmill, it merits more exploration as a conscious choice. Yes, you can compare yourself with others, or you can choose to look at the good, the decent, the beautiful things that life has to offer. In this way, gratitude becomes an intentional practice that engages your selective attention (described in Chapter 1's Mindful Brain Myths).

Still, you might be wondering: How is gratitude powerful enough to overcome the pleasure circuit of the hedonic treadmill? One major reason is that gratitude allows us to *re-value* something, to *re-appreciate* it, so that we don't lose the positive feelings that we once experienced from it. In addition, gratitude affirms the virtuous, beneficial and decent things in the world. If you have gratitude for something, that's incontrovertible evidence that someone else has provided or offered something that you are grateful for, something which allowed you to flourish and grow. It connects you with others, and in this way is a participatory practice that lands you solidly in the here and now.

Instead of living on auto-pilot, grasping for the hedonic highs brought about by materialism, risk, impulse, excitement, and individualism, gratitude finds favor in the vast network of things that support us—from the smallest morsel of food and the farmers in the field to large network of caregivers and others who make such things possible as transportation, housing, and education.

Let's have a look at the four kinds of gratitude that you can begin noticing around you—at home or elsewhere.

1) *Basic Gratitude.* This consists of the little things without which life would be impossible or produce great suffering—such as food, water, shelter, clothes, etc.

2) *Personal Gratitude.* This includes things that enhance your life, such as a job or livelihood, health, a talent or character strength you possess, a car, technology that you use, etc.

3) *Relationship Gratitude.* This highlights all the relationships in your life—whether with persons, the natural world, etc.—that enrich your existence, bring joy, love and feelings of closeness.

4) *Paradoxical Gratitude.* This unusual category—one that humans experience frequently—is about having gratitude for those things you wish you *didn't have* in your life.

Of these, *Paradoxical Gratitude* might at first seem hard to grasp. One of the best stories of paradoxical gratitude that I've heard was shared in a mindfulness workshop that I led in the Midwest. A woman told the story of how her home was totally demolished in a tornado. Prior to the disaster, she had always believed that she was very much alone in the world—even in her own community. This loss pierced her illusion of isolation, as caring people gathered around to help her recover and heal from the traumatic event. That experience, she related, forever changed her by opening her heart to the deep well of goodness that existed in others. We were all very touched by her story, which pointed out how profoundly gratitude can shift our perspective.

EXPERIENCE: RE-VALUING WITH DAILY GRATITUDE

Take a moment to reflect upon these important questions:

- *How has impulsivity of any kind impacted your life or those you are connected with? (This is not to feel bad about, but to simply explore.)*

- *How could you bring greater simplicity into your home life? Could a change in your technology and material needs bring greater peace? If so, how?*

- *What would it be like for you to find one gratitude a day related to home and share that with others? This could also be gratefulness that you feel toward another.*

WHAT'S NEXT:

As you move forward, you might view gratitude as a character strength, a potent means of utilizing intentionality to cope with over-stimulation and to stop living on auto-pilot.

THE BODY SCAN PRACTICE: FINDING SILENCE WITHIN

In recent years, the body scan has been used in therapy and pain clinics to shift—and often reduce—one's perception of pain. In another sense, this ancient practice offers a powerful means of experiencing silence and deep peace by just being fully present, moment-by-moment, with whatever is occurring in the body.

The body scan teaches us how to train the mind to pay attention in a particular way—like a neutral, impassive witness. Thus, while it helps anyone experience pain sensations in a new way, it also teaches how to focus and sustain an open, curious and non-judging attention.

This is a good practice for training that energetic puppy dog mind that constantly wanders off in search of something new. The body scan is a wonderful way to cultivate silence, clarity and a deep open awareness. As Mahatma Gandhi once said:

> *In the attitude of silence*
> *the soul finds the path in a clearer light,*
> *and what is elusive and deceptive*
> *resolves itself into crystal clearness.* [1]

EXPERIENCE: THE BODY SCAN PRACTICE

*Find a quiet place where you can sit or lie down for 5-10 minutes as you follow along with the steps outlined below. (**Please Note**—If you feel discomfort at any time, you can remind yourself that this is simply a sensation. The sensation does not define who you are. **If you suffer from trauma or experience severe discomfort that you feel you can't tolerate, you can always open your eyes and stop.**)*

As you do this practice, use a non-favoring awareness. For example, think of how the colors red, green, blue, or yellow are not innately good or bad; they are just that color. In the same way, a sensation in your body is not innately good or bad, but is just that sensation.

Notice with a sense of openness and curiosity. This means that if there's a pleasant sensation you don't need to hold onto it. Or, if there's an unpleasant sensation, you don't need to avoid, escape or push it away. This awareness isn't taking sides and has no agenda other than to be present and notice.

Step 1: Begin by centering on your body's presence with a couple of deep breaths. Feel your diaphragm move.

Step 2: Inhale, imagining that your breath can carry your awareness to any part of the body, far past the lungs.

Step 3: Bring the breath and awareness into the left foot. Contact any sensation you feel arising, even in the tissue, tendons, ligaments, and bones. After a short time, exhale as you let go of focusing on the foot. With the next in-breath, carry your awareness up to left ankle. Release awareness on the left ankle with an exhalation.

If your puppy dog mind wanders away at any point, that's okay. Just gently bring your attention back to whatever part of the body you were focusing on.

Continue to bring awareness up the body one part at a time, including the lower leg, knee, upper leg, the left hand, left arm and up to the head. Remember to maintain a curious and neutral awareness to whatever is happening moment by moment.

Step 4: After you've moved up one side of the body, slowly move down the other side, sensing each part as you go. If desired, you can combine parts (such as the hip, thigh, knee, calf, shin, and ankle). Optionally, you can include internal organs, the skull, scalp, face, sense organs, and brain.

Step 5: After you've completed scanning the entire body, send a blessing of thanks or gratitude to the body for all it does for you.

Reflect on the following questions:

- *What was your experience of the body scan?*

- *When and how could you incorporate this practice into your daily routine?*

- *How might a short one-minute practice in the morning (upon waking) help get you more connected to the body throughout the day?*

WHAT'S NEXT:

Keep in mind that the body scan practice is not really a relaxation practice, although you might feel more relaxed. As a focused body practice, it's a wonderful meditation for training focus and cultivating a curious and open awareness. Later in this chapter, you'll have an opportunity to put together a daily practice, so consider how the body scan can be part of that.

LOVING-KINDNESS PRACTICE: OPENING TO COMPASSION

The 13th century Persian Poet Rumi once wrote a poem called *The Guest House* in which he compared being human to being like a guest house in which a never-ending stream of changing emotions—from joys to sorrows—would come visiting. "Things don't turn out quite the way we imagine," observes Harvard professor Ronald D. Siegel. "Relationships change and (if we're lucky) our children grow up. Someday the house becomes too small or too big, no longer suiting our needs. We may be shocked to realize that we just borrowed the house for a while and will be passing it on to others. Mindfulness practice helps us to understand the inevitability of these changes from the beginning. Embracing this reality can make it much easier to enjoy the ride, feel less encumbered, and take pleasure in the fleeting moments that constitute our lives. When we allow ourselves to notice the inevitability of change, we relate to our changing bodies and mental faculties differently."[4]

If we can recognize our own aging process and the inevitability of the death that follows, along with the aging experienced by our children and parents, and do so as we embrace the changes that occur in our home, we are well along on the path of accepting life on its own terms rather than trying to live out a fantasy script that we were never meant to control.

This is where compassion and being tender-hearted for others comes into play. To be mindful about aging begins with the release of all negative labels and stigmas which serve to undermine self-esteem in so much of our senior population. One of the pioneering studies in this regard was conducted in 1980 by Ellen J. Langer and Judith Rodin and published in the *Journal of Social Issues.* They brought together a body of research showing how negative labeling ('you are too old to be competent,' for example) and stigmatization of the elderly contributes to attitudes and behaviors that reinforce the stereotypes. Like some self-fulfilling prophecy, when senior citizens accept the prejudice that certain mental and physical limitations must occur, they begin to believe these limitations are already in place and act accordingly.[5]

Mindfulness—and in particular, a loving-kindness practice —creates an internal environment that can better sift out externally induced negativity, particularly the judgments and stereotyping inflicted by others, to give the practitioner a more balanced perspective on the inevitability of mortality and what the aging process really means rather than what they fear it should mean.

Perhaps most importantly, mindful awareness of the nature of impermanence and the inevitability of suffering and loss leads us directly toward the practice of loving-kindness. Loving-kindness acts as a counterbalance to loss and fear by affirming the desire of all living beings to feel safe, secure, understood, and loved. Sharing resources and breathing the same air, we need to be concerned about each other's welfare and well-being. The loving-kindness meditation that follows is meant to extinguish the mistrust and fear that have shadowed humanity for far too long. Loving-kindness recognizes that the only way to survive is to cultivate a deep sense of care and compassion for our fellow beings, and for nature.

Brain research actually shows distinct differences in brains of novices who learn loving-kindness meditation as compared to monks who have been practicing this for many years. In particular, compassion meditation activates synchronous gamma waves—brain waves that are thought to be a sign of high brain function. According to Professor Richard Davidson, who conducted the studies, "most monks showed extremely large increases of a sort that has never been reported before in the neuroscience literature."[6]

Science writer Sharon Begley further explains, "Activity in the left prefrontal cortex (the seat of positive emotions such as happiness) swamped activity in the right prefrontal (site of negative emotions and anxiety), something never before seen from purely mental activity. A sprawling circuit that switches on at the sight of suffering also showed greater activity in the monks. So did regions responsible for planned movement, as if the monks' brains were itching to go to the aid of those in distress."[7]

Knowing how the loving-kindness meditation engages our ability to act on behalf of others is a powerful confirmation of the untapped potential for compassion that lives within us all. Certainly, a compassion practice can help anyone understand why all persons need safety, health, well-being, and happiness.

It's easy to get hardened and frightened in response to impermanence. Compassion and self-compassion are important ways of maintaining a soft, tender and balanced heart, even as the pendulum of change keeps swinging.

EXPERIENCE: LOVING KINDNESS MEDITATION

Read the introductory instructions that follow, then begin with Step 1.

This loving-kindness meditation can prime your brain and body for trust and openness. This ancient practice begins with sending love to your own self. This is not a selfish or me-first kind of love. It is not narcissism. If you have ever loved someone deeply (even a pet), then you know the kind of deep abiding wish for another's safety and well-being that I'm talking about. And so, you will begin by extending this love to yourself.

To give or receive, we must become aware of the boundless potential for love within us so that we can nurture it and replenish it as the circumstances of life and living demand.

Later, you will extend and share this deep wish of love toward others.

Loving kindness can help us to transcend both our smallest and our most dangerous fears. Imagine loving-kindness as a way to give ourselves a great big wonderful hug, and in so doing, change our mood and state of mind for the better so that we project positive feelings to everyone around us.

Step 1:

Begin by sitting in silence, eyes closed, with a focus on your breathing.

When you feel centered, start by forgiving yourself for the hurt you may have caused others. If you have difficulty forgiving yourself as you are today, try picturing yourself as a young child or infant and give forgiveness to that innocent image of yourself.

Now repeat these words to yourself either out loud or inwardly:

> *May I be well.*
> *May I be happy and healthy.*
> *May I be at peace.*
> *May I be free from pain, hunger, and suffering.*

Keep repeating these words to yourself as many times as feels necessary. Let the feeling of love spread into all the cells of your body, even radiating into and from your heart. Continue until the image you hold of yourself is immersed in light and aglow with radiant love. (Some people report feeling warmth, tingling, or other sensations.) If you cannot feel this love, *please do not blame yourself.* Be patient with yourself and the exercise. It sometimes takes time. Don't treat the exercise as some kind of goal to achieve. Treat it as a process, as an approach to life.

Step 2:

Now you can begin to expand your love outward. Start with your family and friends. Picture that person in your mind's eye as radiant and happy and healthy. As you picture that person, repeat the following words either mentally or aloud:

> *May (use their name) be well.*
> *May (name) be happy and healthy.*
> *May (name) be at peace.*
> *May (name) be free from pain, hunger, and suffering.*

After sending loving-kindness to family and friends, you can continue by sending loving-kindness to the following groups:

- mentors, teachers and guides
- neutral persons
- unfriendly persons
- all beings without limitation

When you have finished, place your hands at your heart center and dedicate your blessings for all. Don't be surprised if you feel some strong emotions. Opening to love means opening your tender heart to the world's suffering.

Remember to always send love to yourself first, then to send it outward to others. This is an important practice. It is one that has its greatest benefits if practiced daily. It is a powerful antidote to the self-created suffering that prevents mindfulness from being a moment-by-moment experience of life.

When you are finished, you can complete the practice with these words, which are part of the traditional practice as used in Southeast Asia:

May suffering ones be suffering free.
May the fear struck fearless be.
May grieving ones shed all grief.
May all beings find relief.

Reflect on these questions about your practice:

- *What was your experience of the loving-kindness affirmation?*

- *When and how could you incorporate this practice into your daily life?*

- *How might a short practice in the morning help you foster compassion and understanding through the day?*

WHAT'S NEXT:

The words in this practice can be changed. Adding phrases such as, "May I be safe," "May I be loved," "May I be accepted," or "May I be forgiven," is perfectly fine. Consider using this at times when you feel upset or emotional with another. The loving-kindness practice puts you in touch with the suffering of all beings, and in that way helps to grow compassion for others.

SACRED SPACE AND RITUALS

The last of the practices for inviting mindfulness into heart and home is how you transform your existing space into one that promotes and facilitates your practice. For example, did you ever stop to consider that your home could offer special refuge? That's what a sacred space offers: a quiet and serene place for you to go deeply inward with a mindfulness meditation practice—including some rituals that we'll talk about in a moment. It is here that you can leave worldly demands and pressures behind. It is also here that you enter sacred time—and the vast spaciousness of the here and now.

You can fashion a sacred space to serve your needs and fit your limitations. The sacred space can be a closet, the corner of a room, or an entire room. While it could even be your entire living space, let's begin by creating a distinct space within your home that you select with care. Try to find a spot that limits both noise and ambient light. The corner of a large closet is often ideal. If that doesn't work for you, find a room and clear out a corner, then erect a folding screen around the space to give you some privacy. The space needs to be just large enough for you to sit, either on the floor or in a chair, in a comfortable position.

It might help to have objects in front of you that are meaningful. You could think of this as an altar, or just a reminder of what you deeply value and care about. In some religious traditions, an altar is a surface on which to place sacred objects for veneration. For our purposes, these objects don't need to have any special religious or spiritual significance, though that will work if you so choose. Meaningful objects can be photographs of your children, or images of people (current or historical) who have had an important impact on your character development or values as a human being.

Such objects can also be spiritual books, poetry, or mementos from your past that have special symbolic significance for you. You can even write out vows and intentions on pieces of paper and place them in a bowl before you. The point is to have objects resting before you which give you a focus for contemplation, and that can help to ground you for your mindfulness meditations. Just be careful that what you choose to place on your altar serves to focus your awareness rather than to distract it.

Once your sacred space is created, consider making it an interruption-free zone, a place just for you to experience peace. That is part of what makes it both sacred and special. In this way, you set a mood that facilitates quicker and deeper immersion into the meditation each time you enter this special domain. Silence does not have to be found at home, but your sacred space can be a good place to start.

Elisabeth Kübler-Ross, a pioneer in the field of death and dying, talked about finding the silence that is all around: "There is no need to go to India," she said, "or anywhere else to find peace. You will find that deep place of silence right in your room, your garden or even your bathtub."[2]

Silence is a special gift that comes wrapped in many shapes and packages. How you invite this into your life is as unique as you are. Here are a few tips about finding silence:

- Consciously spend time in nature as a way to limit electronic noise and distractions.
- Get quiet so you can notice the mind's activity—its thoughts, emotions, cravings and desires.
- Go on a technology diet for part of the day, where you turn off the computer, phone, television, etc.
- Practice some form of ritual with your family and/or children—such as a taking a moment for silence or sharing gratitude at mealtime.

Would you believe that electronic noise and multi-tasking can actually lower a person's IQ? A British study found that test subjects who tried to juggle all of this input actually experienced a loss of up to 10 points in their IQ scores.[3] But why not see for yourself what changes can shift your experience and bring you into a more satisfying and natural pace of life.

Mindfulness as a Ritual

You might not think of mindfulness as a ritual practice, but anything that you repeat in an intentional, planned and purposeful way that organizes and disciplines your thoughts and actions can be considered a ritual.

Unspoken rituals abound in daily life. How you greet others with a "hello" and shake hands is a ritual. Similarly, how you prepare for bed and what you say to others at nighttime is a form of ritual. Giving thanks or saying grace before meal is a ritual. Basically, rituals bring a sense of order to living. They smooth our way by helping us know how to act or what to expect.

In your sacred space, you will create an intentional form of practice, or a ritual, that best suits you. Keep in mind that you can just as easily view your workspace as a sacred space, placing items and using practices to generate positive and helpful rituals. In the experience below, let's explore how to create a sacred space and what practice you might use there.

EXPERIENCE: CREATING SACRED SPACE AND RITUAL PRACTICE

Answer the questions below to explore what sacred space and ritual might look like for you.

Part 1: Creating a Sacred Space

- *How filled up is your life with busy-ness? What are the challenges you face in bringing silence into your home, even if for a short while?*

- *What is one way that you could create more simplicity and silence in your home?*

- *Where in your living space could you create a sacred mindfulness space? What might this look like? What objects might be present to make this space special?*

PART 2: CREATING A RITUAL PRACTICE

- *What mindfulness practices have appealed to you thus far? What do you hope a ritual can accomplish for you? —such as disciplining your mindfulness meditation practice, finding peace by resting the weary mind, or getting in touch with compassion, etc.*

- *Write down the procedure or steps you might use upon first entering your sacred space, such as bowing, putting your hands over the heart center or taking a conscious breath.*

- *What practice(s) will you use in your sacred space? Feel free to change these practices as you learn what works best for you.*

WHAT'S NEXT:

Over the next week, take time to look over your ideas about creating a sacred space. You needn't rush out and create the space immediately. Try sitting in different locations in your home until you find the one that feels right and helps you settle in. Have fun as you collect the objects and items that resonate with you. Then, when you feel ready, set a time to start putting together your actual sacred space.

As for beginning a mindfulness practice, try starting with an amount of time that is *small, realistic* and *achievable*. Even if you begin with a three-minute breathing practice, that is a good place to start. Keep in mind that building up your practice is a lot like going to the gym. It takes time, and the changes occur incrementally. But after a month or two you'll start to notice the difference.

MINDFUL TRANSITION POINTS AND RITUALS FOR HOME

In the last chapter, we explored several workday transition points. Let's do the same now for the home, based on the idea that you can intentionally develop supportive rituals that transform mundane time into mindful moments.

- **Waking Up**

How you wake up can set the rhythm for your day. Some people like to practice the body scan practice as a way to get centered soon after waking. Showering, brushing your teeth, and dressing can be mindful practices if you step out of automatic mode. This can be accomplished, for example, by using your non-dominant hand for tasks like brushing your teeth. As you collect your presence, such as by feeling the drops of water in the shower, you also selectively restrain the mind from moving off toward future thoughts and anxieties.

- **Leaving for Work**

If you are leaving for work or for another purpose, how you use a goodbye ritual with those in your home brings a sense of meaning to the relationships. You may decide to set a conscious intention for what you hope to accomplish during your day.

- **Returning Home from Work**

Natural transition points happen when you either leave or return from your home. If your transition point is from work to home, try to find ways to decompress and distress during your commute home. For some, this transition point could be time to listen to calming music, breathe, or listen to books on tape.

Arriving home, transition out of work clothes and into your casual and relaxing "home" attire. Another ritual means of transitioning is to use the soothing power of water to dissolve negative energy by taking a hot bath or shower. Even splashing water on your face and hands can be calming and relaxing.

- **Greeting Family Members**

How do you greet your partner and/or children when you come home? Do you shut off the computer or technology so you can greet them with a loving hug or kiss? What is your mood state? Are you able to show excitement at seeing them? Or do you immediately point out something that is wrong or unfinished (homework, the chores)? Make a conscious effort to relate in a meaningful and loving way—perhaps opening the space for you to share time together.

- **Pets**

If you have a cat or dog as a companion, playing with your

pet or walking your pet can act as a morning or evening transition ritual during which you can enjoy the outdoors. Pets often look at you with rapt attention. Give them the same courtesy of your full and compassionate attention in return.

• Leaving and Returning

Even those times that you leave and then re-enter your home to run errands are transition points. You can create mindful rituals around these exits and entries. You might, for example, state your intention each time you cross a "threshold," which is every time you go through a door. You can recite a short prayer or repeat words of safety when you or a loved one ventures into the outside world. When you or a loved one returns, say a short blessing of thanks for the return.

• Meals

Perhaps one of the most nourishing transition rituals is the meal you share with family or friends. This is a transition point with the potential for meaning and joy. Mealtime rituals are important in all traditions. In the Japanese Tea Ceremony, for example, all of the objects used in making and drinking the tea —the delicate bamboo whisk, iron tea kettle, and the beautifully designed teacups—are all passed around and appreciated with a sense of thankfulness and gratitude.

You can easily bring a mindful approach to your meals. Start by beautifying the dinner table. Invite nature in with a flower arrangement. Spend time simply noticing the colors or aromas of the foods as you prepare the meal. You could, for example, prepare a special meal once a week in which the entire preparation period becomes a mindful ritual.

Before eating, contemplate all of the time and energy that went into creating this food—the water, the sunlight, the soil nutrients, and the vast network of people who planted, cultivated, and made this food available for your enjoyment.

There are hundreds of books with food blessings from around the world that you can adapt as a way to create your own grace. Remember, though, that you don't need to say a formal grace with your meal to make it mindful or spiritual. Sometimes simply spicing your meal with gratitude can be enough to make your experience of food more meaningful and an opportunity to create new levels of bonding within the family.

Try eating each bite of your meal with slow and methodical attention to every sensation of taste and texture in the food. Savor what you put into your mouth. You could set aside a meal each week or month in which you and your family eat slowly in total silence. You might be surprised at what can happen when you create such a mindful and peaceful environment. At the end of the meal, when conversation is allowed again, you may find that the subject matter and emotional content is deeper and more meaningful than what your family might normally experience.

• Sleep

Recharging your batteries with sleep after a long day is one of the most important transition points in your life. There are many ways to prepare for and care for this transition point. Your body naturally wants to sleep, and this requires setting boundaries around your mindful sleep practice: allow yourself to wind down for an hour before sleep; keep your sleeping space dark and quiet; standardize the time you go to sleep; maintain boundaries from friends and others who call/text/e-mail at all hours of the night.

EXPERIENCE: HOME TRANSITION POINTS

Reflect on the following questions:

- *Which home-related transition points are the most stressful or difficult for you to manage?*

- *What is an important transition point that would benefit from mindfulness and improve relationships at home?*

- *What additional transition points can you think of that you face at home or in family relationships?*

- *What activities (such as exercise, stretching, meditating) can act as transitions to help you locate balance in your life? When and how could you best practice these?*

WHAT'S NEXT:

With the ideas and practices in this chapter, you are building a solid foundation of practices, along with a structure for implementing them. You can always invite self-hospitality and kindness should things not turn out as planned. That's the beauty of mindfulness—it's actually *re-mindfulness* that gently nudges us to change course as needed.

~

Key Chapter References

1. Fishel, R. (2008) *Peace in Our Hearts, Peace in the World: Meditations of Hope and Healing.* New York: Sterling.

2. Cashman, K. (2008) *Leadership from the Inside Out: Becoming a Leader for Life.* San Francisco: Berrett-Koehler Publishers.

3. "Emails 'Hurt IQ More Than Pot,'" http://cnn.com/2005/WORLD/europe/04/22/text.iq/ (accessed Dec. 2019).

4. Siegel, R.D. (2010) *The Mindfulness Solution.* New York: Guilford Press.

5. Rodin, J., Langer, E.J. (1980) Aging Labels: The decline of control and the fall of self-esteem. *Journal of Social Issues.* 1980; 36(2):12-29.

6. Begley, S. (2004) Scans of Monks' Brains Show Meditation Alters Structure, Functioning. *The Wall Street Journal.* 2004 Nov. 5; B1.

7. same as 6.

6

REFLECTION AND THE POWER OF PAUSE

*T*he ability to pause and reflect inwardly is being lost in our modern, fast-paced world. Our attention is constantly being directed toward screens of all shapes and sizes. There seems to be little time or inclination to go inward, which is how we wisely discern, think about who we are, and decide what matters most to us. Pausing to reflect enhances the ability learn, which is why metacognition—the process of introspectively appraising what one has learned and monitoring one's behavior—has long been a central tool in educational theory and practice.[1]

It should come as no surprise that metacognition has been linked to meditation. In a study conducted at the University of California, researchers taught a two-week meditation-training program to individuals to see how this would impact their "introspective accuracy" in areas such as perception and memory. Subjects who underwent the meditation program showed significant improvements in memory accuracy compared to those who did not get the training. This interesting study points out that meditation improves our ability to reflect inwardly.[2]

As mentioned in Chapter 1, the prefrontal cortex of the brain makes possible mindfulness, metacognition, social connection, and empathy. I like to think of this as the *reflect and relate module* of the brain. Strengthening this part of the brain is an indispensable part of being human. Without an engaged reflect and relate module, we might simply become conditioned widgets reduced to algorithms designed by artificial intelligence that parse our behavior in order to get us to do their bidding.

Now, I'm not suggesting you ditch technology. It's an inescapable and helpful part of our lives. (In full disclosure, this book was written with technology useful for researching and writing, for which I'm grateful.) We use technology for banking, checking in at the hospital, in our workplaces, staying connected to friends and family, and so much more. At the same time, it's worth reflecting on these questions: How much is technology pulling me away from my essence and the essence of others? How is it impeding my capacity to access the full potential of human awareness?

That's exactly why we need an evolved Mindfulness for the 21st Century—a simple, accessible, and transformative practice to use throughout the day. As you've been reading this book, you may feel you don't have time for some of the practices here. Even though I have tried to make these practices adaptable, and even brief, that could be challenging for some. This is where a portable and deep awareness practice of daily reflection comes into play.

REFLECTION: MINDFULNESS FOR THE 21ST CENTURY

Remember yourself always and everywhere.[3]
—*Gurdjieff*

Before jumping in, let's explore the idea of reflection a little more. The Latin root for the word reflection means "to bend back"–such as a mirror bending back your image to you. But we can also "bend back" our thoughts, our senses, our emotions, and even distracted awareness in order to come back to the here and now, get off auto pilot, and gain new insights. We've all heard of persons who reflected on their lives and underwent a dramatic transformation–such as John Newton, who transformed from being a slave ship captain to a minister devoted to freeing slaves. The words he penned for *Amazing* Grace have endured for centuries.

> *Amazing Grace! How sweet the sound*
> *That saved a wretch like me.*
> *I once was lost, but now am found,*
> *Was blind, but now I see.*[4]

Such is the power of reflection. Although reflection offers all the same benefits of mindfulness meditation, you might think of it as a lightning strike that instantly floods the mind's darkness and confusion with brilliance. This is not unlike the purpose of kōans—those short stories or poems in the Zen tradition meant to elicit intuitive insight.

And yet, there's another important reason to reflect. Imagine encountering a pool of water with so much turbulence at the surface that it's impossible to see anything reflected off the water's surface. Now, imagine finding a second pool–but the water in this pond is perfectly still, so everything reflects off of it–the clouds, the trees, the sun, and so on. Reflection stills the mind so that it can achieve greater clarity and calm. The unruffled mind allows you to have a more spacious view of what's happening around you, rather than getting pulled in to reactivity.

In *Freedom from the Known*, spiritual teacher J. Krishnamurti affirmed the transforming power of meditation:

Meditation is one of the greatest arts in life — perhaps the *greatest, and one cannot possibly learn it from anybody, that is the beauty of it. It has no technique and therefore no authority. When you learn about yourself, watch yourself, watch the way you walk, how you eat, what you say, the gossip, the hate, the jealousy — if you are aware of all that in yourself, without any choice, that is part of meditation.*

So, meditation can take place when you are sitting in a bus or walking in the woods full of light and shadows, or listening to the singing of birds or looking at the face of your wife or child.[5]

∼

REFLECTION: FINDING TRUTH AND FREEDOM

Through a reflect practice we 1) build concentrative awareness in order to see the true nature of mind and ego, 2) recognize those things that we cling or attach to (as well as avoid) that cause us and others suffering, 3) strengthen intentionality and ethical behavior, and 4) free ourselves from suffering by growing in joy, compassion and love and laughter–and step onto a path where each day is purposeful, precious and meaningful.

To reflect is to experience the full expression of mindfulness.

This is real liberation—from illusion and suffering—that can only be revealed by penetrating the nature of mind, of ego, of impermanence, of attachment and avoidance. Reflection cuts through the illusion of self, for if we don't first disarm the ego in order to make peace with ourselves, how can we hope to make peace with others? How can we cultivate nurturing and enriching relationships?

Reflection is unlike the analytical thought we typically use when trying to solve or fix problems. If you've ever found yourself going around and around in a circle trying to solve a problem, you know how frustrating and unhelpful that can be. For example, I entered the monastery because of painful patterns that kept repeating in my life. I wanted to peer more deeply to discover the causes in order to untie and loosen those old knots.

As you might imagine, that process took a lot of time. But what I've distilled from years of sitting meditation is that *it's not the length of time that you spend looking inwardly that matters. It's knowing which concise and targeted reflections* will absolutely break through old, toxic patterns. When you do this, it enables you to go beyond unproductive thinking in a short period of time. This is the equivalent of having the right key to unlock a particular door.

Just pausing for a minute or two to reflect throughout the day re-collects your fragmented parts so you can know the truth and wholeness of presence.

Interestingly, reflection is the *opposite of trying.* As a deep, penetrating awareness, its purpose is to precisely help us go beyond traditional forms of thinking. Don't be surprised if you gain fresh insights, creative solutions, and new awareness to relationships and your work. So, it's not so much *what* you reflect on, but *how* you bring a fresh and abiding awareness to any area of your life that matters.

Reflection is a practice of full presence that refines and develops insight and innersight awareness. The reflections in this chapter are just a small taste of the 108 reflections found in my book, *Reflect: Awaken to the Wisdom of the Here and Now.* Each of these reflections nurtures the multi-dimensional awareness necessary for manifesting a deep sense of clarity and wisdom. What is different in these pages, however, is that you will learn a four-part structure for using reflection. This structure is described below.

How to Reflect Using the Prrr Method

As you use the following reflections, you'll be practicing a method of Pause, Reflect, Relate and Repeat throughout the day. I call this Prrr (like a cat). Let's look at each of these steps more closely.

- PAUSE: Any time during the day when you feel overwhelmed, stuck in rumination or feel like you are sleep walking through the moment, just physically stop and pause. Take a nice breath or two to get present and centered.
- REFLECT: Recall one of the reflections, or readings, that are in this chapter. Bring yourself back to the core idea or theme of that reading, and allow yourself to look inward.

Since each reflection is followed by three probing questions, or prompts, you can bring your awareness to one of those questions. Keep in mind that a reflection practice is done without expectation of getting anything in return, but just allowing yourself to surrender to whatever insights or wisdom may come to you. Stay with the breath as you do this, feeling how nice it is to slow down for a few moments.

- RELATE: After reflecting, gently broaden your awareness to those around you. How does your reflection help you to understand or have greater insight into others–their predicaments, their uniqueness, etc.?

Allow yourself in the moment to soften, to see others as fellow travelers in this life journey who need support, as we all do. Allow yourself to act with compassion and wisdom should the opportunity arise.

- REPEAT: Remember to repeat this process by giving yourself a *reflect break* as needed throughout the day. Take as many of these as needed, even if it's just to slow down and be present with the body and the breath.

Our first reflection will be on the subject of simplicity and peace because these are vital to our wellbeing at many levels. There's that peace we have with our own mind. And there's the simplicity that comes from appreciating the simple, ordinary things. Below, you will be reading a reflection that focuses on creating peace with the mind.

Before beginning, I'd like you to consider the following question: Did you count the number of thoughts you had today? (I didn't think so, but then that's a rhetorical question!)

The number of thoughts a person can have has been estimated at about 25 thoughts per minute, which seems like a pretty conservative estimate. Now, when you multiply this for the course of a day, you'd have over 20,000 thoughts a day. Now, for a moment ask yourself these questions:

How many of those 20,000 thoughts tell you something really profound about who you are?
How many of these thoughts are even accurate?

In truth, most of our thoughts are conditioned, repetitive, reactive, habitual, or random. Yet because these thoughts come from *inside our own head* we sometimes take them a lot more seriously than they deserve. As an example of this, I once had a client write down several of the thoughts in his head that he believed were true about him. After completing the list, I asked him if I could read the statements out loud. He said, "sure," and when I read his words aloud verbatim, he started laughing.

"What's so funny?" I asked.

"It just occurred to me that if I heard somebody else saying those things—well, I'd think it was the most ridiculous thing in the world!"

If you find that you sometimes have a war going on inside your mind–pulling you this way and that–join the club. That's why our first reflection is designed to help you to become better "friends" with your mind by getting to know it up close and personal.

EXPERIENCE: NURTURING SIMPLICITY AND PEACE

Find a time or place where it's quiet. Begin by getting present in the body and taking a few calming breaths. There are two steps to follow:

Familiarize Yourself with the Reading.

As you read, imagine these are words that you could have written. You might even read them in a whispered tone, inviting silence as you do so. Repeat the passage as often as you want, letting its meaning seep into all your cells.

Sit without expectation, but simply surrendering yourself to the meaning within. See if there's a line or phrase that pulls you in. If so, you might decide to repeat that line or phrase over and over. Then, come to rest as you "reflect on this."

It's impossible to hold onto a river,
but you can flow with it.

Feelings and thoughts are droplets
in an endless river
flowing out to the ocean.

None are final,
so why hold onto dissolving droplets?
Instead, watch them flow past and through.
This is nature's way,
and the way to find peace
with feelings and thoughts.

Reflect on this.

Reflect and Journal

You can reflect on your own, and also use the three questions, or targeted prompts below. These are designed to take you more deeply into reflection. Remember to use the Prrr practice, Pause-Reflect-Relate-Repeat. Also know that there are no right or wrong answers to your reflection. Allow yourself to open to whatever may come to you. Let's begin:

- *What is it like to observe—just for one minute—how quickly thoughts and feelings change?* (Imagine that you're watching a scary movie when the lights in the theatre suddenly come on. When you look back to see how the images are simply projections from the projector, you're no longer frightened. In the same way, you're turning on the lights in the theatre of your mind.)

- *How can noticing this flow be useful?* (You may notice certain themes that arise. What is it like for you to become more aware of thoughts and feelings in this way? Remember that you don't need to judge

133

thoughts harshly. Picture them as a mindstream of mental droplets flowing out to the ocean.)

• *For one day, what is it like to be a keen observer of your thoughts, watching them pass by as fleeting and temporary visitors?*

WHAT'S NEXT:

What was this first experience of using a brief reflection like for you? How could you incorporate this into your day by pausing, reflecting, relating and repeating? Moving forward, consider what would be a good time for you to do a reflect reading—morning, midday, evening? Think about this as a ritual for deepening your practice and softening your heart.

The work you are doing here is a path of self-evolution, one that actually changes how you process and experience thoughts. Once you start a reflect practice, you'll probably wonder how you ever got along without it. You bring awareness to everything one way or another, but when you reflect you bring a deeper sensitivity and openness to each moment, each interaction you have—with yourself and others.

REFLECTING ON EMOTIONS

For this next experience, we're going to reflect on something that can be challenging–our emotions. Even though I have been practicing traditional meditation, mindfulness and reflect practices for years, I'm often surprised at how loudly my mind will still react emotionally to a particular situation. That's because the brain is profoundly emotional.

Sometimes, I find this hilarious and actually laugh at my own inner mental contortions. Other times, I need to go deeper in order to understand what has caused these "knots" to reappear in my life. How can I begin to untie them, ever so gently and with self-compassion? It helps to remember that everyone has been wounded or harmed in some way. And, we all deserve compassion and understanding. As you practice today's reflection, keep in mind that we don't want to banish or eliminate difficult emotions, but rather to honor and appreciate them as part of our history.

In terms of brain science, there are fibers running between the pre-frontal cortex (the reflect module) and the amygdala (the survival center). That means that when you reflect on and observe your emotions, you're actually integrating the more ancient emotional part of the brain—which is shared by all mammals—with the more advanced executive center.

A pause practice is exactly what helps you step back from *grabbing on and reacting* to an emotion (or a craving). That's because when you pause, that emotion becomes the *object of your attention*. You're observing it with a sense of curiosity and kindness. In other words, you've literally *changed your relationship* to the emotion. In turn, this process rewires the brain's pathways, which also changes how you will think and react to emotions in the future.

The good news is that even a few minutes of reflection each day can change subtle neural pathways.

EXPERIENCE: REFLECTION ON EMOTIONS

As before, find a time or place where it's quiet. Begin by getting present in the body and taking a few calming breaths.

Part 1: Familiarize Yourself with the Reading

Again, imagine these are words that you could have written. It might help to speak the words softly, repeating the passage as its meaning is absorbed.

Sit without any expectation as you enter an open space of non-trying and non-desiring. If a line or phrase speaks to you, you might repeat that line or phrase over and over.

Invite your unwanted emotions
inside for a cup of tea.

Do you try to avoid negative emotions?
Yes, you can have your mental police
handcuff and put unwanted feelings
in a paddy wagon never to be seen again.

Or, you can invite them inside for a cup of tea.

What is the message behind the emotions?
Are you out of balance, needing rest,
needing safe boundaries, needing simplicity?

Before you call the police, have a cup of tea.
You may discover the supreme blessing
you've been waiting for.

Reflect on this.

Part 2: Reflect and Journal

As before, you can either journal or just inwardly reflect on these questions. You can do this now, or you can carry the reading and reflections with you. I prefer the latter method because it encourages and reinforces using the Prrr practice throughout the day. Most importantly, you'll be strengthening the reflect and relate module of the brain as you slow down, get present and build caring relationships.

- *How willing are you to invite unwanted emotions into your life?* (Remember that the purpose of this practice is not to blame yourself for your emotions. You are just getting curious about them.)

- *What emotions would it help to invite in for a cup of tea and why?* (You might want to recall a time when you've avoided certain emotions. Choose one that stands out, and allow yourself to consider the role of that emotion in your life.)

- *Today, have a cup of tea with unwanted feelings. What new understanding is offered by doing this?*

WHAT'S NEXT:

It takes courage to look at your emotions, and I hope you have gained some new insights from this practice. This means we don't need to fear emotions. They have a lot to share with us if only we take the time to listen in with kindness and a willingness to learn.

You can find poems, scripture and meaningful readings from many sources to use as reflections. Here's one about emotions, written by meditation teacher Frank Coppieters from his book, *Handbook for the Evolving Heart*:

> *Remember, the path is never as arduous*
> *as it looks–only resistance makes it so.* [6]

REFLECTION ON THE PRECIOUS ORDINARY

Think back on your day for a moment. Were there any little, ordinary moments that you just let pass by or took for granted? What if these moments possessed more meaning and joy than you imagined? That's what researchers found when they studied students who were told to chronicle an extraordinary event (a romantic date) and an ordinary event. These records were stored by the researchers. Then, three months later, the subjects were asked to review and rate their previous extraordinary and ordinary events. The results showed that the subjects rated the daily, mundane events as more interesting than the extraordinary one. This led researchers to conclude that, "people are likely to underestimate the pleasure of rediscovering ordinary mundane experiences." [7]

A more poetic and sublime way of viewing the ordinary moment comes from contemplative Gunilla Norris, who writes:

> *Help me to not be so afraid*
> *of the heights and depths! Help me*
> *to concentrate on the connection*
> *between the two: those humble steps,*
> *Those one-after-the-other steps,*
> *which are the only ones I can really take.*
> *Help me to love a slow progression,*
> *To have no prejudice*
> *that up is better than down or vice versa.*
> *Help me to enjoy the in-between.* [8]

We make judgements all the time as we experience the

moment. Those judgements are filters that may either add to or subtract from what is really occurring. Rather than being fixed on the outcome, we can notice each step of the journey, which requires a "slow progression." As a result, we start to notice those small pleasant moments of joy. In fact, research in the positive psychology field shows that a practice known as "savoring"— spending time remembering good past experiences—is a powerful means of increasing positive emotional affect and mood.

You might think of this as "bending back" or reflecting back to yourself those positive memories, so to speak. This is another important aspect of a reflect practice, and one that we'll use here.

EXPERIENCE: REFLECTION ON THE PRECIOUS ORDINARY

As before, find a quiet place where you won't be interrupted. Begin by getting present in the body and taking a few nice, soothing breaths.

Part 1: Familiarize Yourself with the Reading

Sit with spaciousness, opening to the heart and the world.

Goals are just momentary
punctuation points on a bigger journey.

It's not just when you arrive that counts,
but how you get there.
If your goal-oriented perfectionist is pushing you,
simply smile back.

Remind yourself about
those in-between moments,

those little heart-filled moments along the way
that make any goal memorable.

After all,
the period at the end of the sentence
is no more important than the other letters.
It is only one character on your keyboard.
(And typos are sure to hippen.)

Reflect on this.

Part 2: Reflect and Journal

- *How can you appreciate and tune in to the in-between moments?*

- *What might happen if you steeped yourself in the journey and worried less about the goal?*

- *What would it be like for to you invite greater forgiveness and kindness to yourself as you move toward any goal? What would one action in that direction look like?*

- *Today, release one outcome so that you can focus on the journey. What is an in-between moment you might enjoy?*

WHAT'S NEXT:

May you find many new ordinary treasures in today's practice of noticing and slowing down. Being under constant time pressure and deadlines is another kind of suffering, isn't it? By giving yourself more space and time to be with the little moments, you may find that everything gets done anyway. Or, as I have written in *Reflect,* "Don't get lost in the future. You'll get there anyway, without even trying."

REFLECTION ON BEING FAITHFUL TO YOURSELF

What does the idea of "bliss" mean to you? You may imagine it as some transcendental state of being, like floating on a cloud, without a worry in the world. But bliss can be a simple shift in awareness that transforms the mundane into the sublime. Bliss, for example, can be having gratitude in your life. It is noticing tranquility and contentment. It is the feeling of self-awareness and acceptance for the whole parts of ourselves–even those shadow sides that are hidden from sight. Bliss is even being here, reading this, because you feel alive and are utilizing your capacity to find meaning.

That brings us to the next reflection, which is the bliss of being faithful to yourself, and recognizing the beauty and gifts which you have been given. As the Taoist sage Lao Tzu wrote:

> *Be content with what you have,*
> *rejoice in the way things are.*
> *When you realize there is nothing lacking,*
> *the whole world belongs to you.* [9]

Finding contentment means overcoming negative mental states–such as envy, hatred, anger, jealousy, and greed–that diminish or devalue your sense of well-being. This is very much in line with the ancient practice of mindfulness, whose purpose is to recognize and overcome the emotional poisons that keep us unhappily entangled.

In fact, feelings of peace and acceptance for yourself and concern for others are incompatible with negative emotions that arise when you are focused on comparing and grasping for what others have. It's hard to feel bad toward someone for what they have if you accept yourself fully and are grateful for what's in your life. It's a very different way of existing in the world, isn't it? Best of all, by appreciating your own gifts, you are ready to act in a way that delivers your very best to others.

How sublime!

EXPERIENCE: REFLECTION ON BEING FAITHFUL TO YOURSELF

Settle in with quietude and presence, taking a few nice, soothing breaths.

Part 1: Familiarize Yourself with the Reading

Bring open-heartedness to each unfolding moment as you read these words.

> *Better to be the oak tree you are*
> *than the palm tree you aren't.*

> *If you really want to be miserable,*
> *first compare yourself to others.*
> *Then focus on what others have,*
> *and what's missing from your life.*

> *The oak tree wanting to be as skinny*
> *as a palm tree is one very unhappy tree.*

Be faithful to yourself.
Each tree is beautiful, unique.
Be true to yourself in order to
get free of envy, jealousy, and greed.

Such is joy and bliss.

Reflect on this.

Part 2: Reflect and Journal

As before, journal in the space below, reflect, or use the Prrr method during your day.

- *How does comparison with the situation, status, or condition of others diminish or harm you?* (Whatever others may have told you, whatever beliefs you have come to hold about yourself, there is a lot more to you than meets the eye.)

- *How would it feel to appreciate yourself for who you are and what you've been given?* (Drop the busy analytic mind and come into the body and appreciate your many gifts, all the unique attributes that make you who you are. Just sense this, knowing that a human existence is a precious and rare thing in the Universe.)

- *Right now, name one unique thing about yourself that you can accept. How can you cultivate and celebrate yourself with greater acceptance?* (If you are worried about

143

accepting something you don't want in your life, remember this saying: "I'm perfect just as I am, *and* I could use a little improvement." This reflection's purpose is to find the bliss of not being stuck in rigid thinking about ourselves. How does it feel to let in these previously unwanted parts of yourself?)

WHAT'S NEXT:

This reflection practice is one that I encourage you to continue to use often. This is one way we *re-member, re-collect* and even *re-appreciate* those fragmented and lost parts of ourselves.

REFLECTION ON RELATIONSHIPS

One of the misconceptions of mindfulness is that it is primarily about noticing what comes through the sense doors and being aware of thoughts and emotions and the body. If that were all mindfulness represented, it would be a very lonely and isolated mindfulness. Mindfulness is very much steeped in how we co-create our world through our inter-relationships with persons, the air, the water, the planet, the plants, and all creatures. In our western culture, it's commonplace to place a high value on our independence.

This illusion of independence was lifted for me when I was in the monastery and had my first meal with the monks. All the food was brought in and offered to us by a nearby community of Burmese people. I was humbled by this gracious act of caring, and by the realization that even the smallest morsel on our plates comes from the vast interwoven network of being—the sunshine, the rain, natural nutrients and human effort. This helped me develop gratitude for all those persons and things—

seen and unseen—without which life would be extremely difficult if not impossible. It's good to see that researchers quantifying the importance of our social contacts.

To understand the effects of social relationships on our health, researchers at Brigham Young University analyzed almost 150 previously published studies about human interaction and health. These were all longitudinal studies, and the outcomes they tracked averaged over seven years. The data found that when individuals were more integrated into and connected with a group, they were more likely to take care of others, take care of themselves, and take fewer risks. How does the lack of a robust social connection compare with other mortality risks? The findings from this study were stark: When compared to other risk factors, a lack of a strong social network was shown to be as bad as smoking 15 cigarettes a day or being alcoholic. In addition, it produced a worse health outcome than not exercising and was twice as bad as obesity.[10]

Other studies have found that over the past two decades Americans have become increasingly isolated. There was one study that showed when you go to bed lonely or sad at night, that when you awaken your body will receive a higher jolt of cortisol.[11] It's as if your body is listening in on your social and emotional experiences and is preparing you for what it feels is a stressful day because you lack the necessary support. As you may recall from Chapter 1, chronic stress and the cortisol that results puts the brakes on the immune system. This is more evidence why developing nurturing relationships is important.

Creating mutually positive and satisfying relationships takes a lot of work and time. Some believe the answer is found by expecting others to change. Such persons might say, "If only my partner would do things the right way, the way I like them done, then we wouldn't have any problems!" Well, that may be true, but I'm not sure you'd call that a mutual relationship.

Instead of expecting others to do the heavy lifting, we're

going to look at the things that *we* bring to a relationship. These are the things we can control and change–such as toxic patterns and habitual habits that get in the way of building mutual, kind relationships. You might be surprised how this alone can have an effect on others.

No single reflection is a magic bullet. Because we all have relationship "blind spots," the following reflection will have us looking within and noticing our own "messy can of worms"– which you can think of as all the entrenched ideas, beliefs and behaviors that each of us carries around. The point is that you don't need to let your worms eat their way into the fruits of a potentially beautiful and loving relationship. After all, you know what a single worm can do to an apple!

Remember to maintain self-kindness and self-compassion as you do this practice. Everyone has worms, so you don't need to blame yourself or shame yourself because of this. Besides, your "worms" are a part of your past and your history, which you can honor and appreciate.

You may even feel a loss at letting go of your worms. That's okay too. If anything, you can feel good that you are finding your worms a new home as you move forward in a new direction.

EXPERIENCE: REFLECTION ON OUR RELATIONSHIP WORMS

Settle in with full presence and a few breaths.

Part 1: Familiarize Yourself with the Reading

Invite a spacious mind and heart. Read this over as many times as you want. You may even find a phrase or word that speaks to you.

Everyone owns a big,
messy can of worms.

When relationship problems repeat,
causing hurt, anger, and frustration, who's to blame?
Maybe no one.
Maybe it's just those two big cans of worms.

But before you blame the other person's worms,
look at your own worms first.
How do you keep feeding them,
keeping them plump and alive?

You don't need to fight or kill the worms.
Just take them out of your home
and put them back in the garden.
They'll be happier there, and so will you.

Reflect on this.

Part 2: Reflect and Journal

Journal in the space below or reflect. It's also recommended that you *Prrr* throughout your day.

- *What relationship "worms" follow you around?* (This can be a rigid belief, an old idea, a behavior, an expectation of others that you hold onto? Noticing just one "worm" is good enough, but you may notice more than one.)

- *How can you move forward and still honor your past worm(s)?* (You might even consider having a "talk" or dialogue with your worms, thanking them for how they may have been useful or protected you in the past, but are no longer required.)

- *How can you stop feeding your worms today?* (What new behavior, belief, or expectation can you let go of today? What will this look like in your relationship? How can you continue to nurture mutual and loving ways of relating?)

WHAT'S NEXT:

It takes courage to reflect and peer into your relationship worms. I hope you can move them into the garden. Even though this process takes time, you've taken an important step toward clearing away inner roadblocks to sustainable relationships. Have patience with yourself... and your worms. As you awaken yourself, your relationships will magically seem to awaken as well.

Keep on the lookout for readings that can help you reflect, that can aid in loosening some of the karmic or historic knots that keep you bound in old behaviors and beliefs. In the next chapter, we'll wrap things up by exploring how to move forward with mindfulness.

But first, here are four more reflections that I wanted to share with you from *Reflect: Awaken to the Wisdom of the Here and Now*. These speak to the topics of presence, love, compassion and awakening.

*Stop watching the clock, and wade in
the pool of the timeless now.*

*Present-moment awareness is void of
conventional time.*

*The timeless Here and Now is your personal pool,
waiting for you to jump in
and take a refreshing swim.*

*Right now, stop. Look around.
Be present with your surroundings,
your body,
your breath,
all your senses,
and the conscious mind.
Awareness itself.*

*You can always enter the pool of endless,
timeless Now.*

Reflect on this.

*Don't wait another moment to send
the warm smile of love inward.*

*Since no one gets the perfect parent,
why not play the role of being
your own best parent and friend?*

Acknowledge that you are doing your best.

Make time to pause,
inhaling the warm glow
of self-acceptance and self-appreciation.

Agree to make peace with whoever is in there.

Only then, can you make peace
with whoever is out there.

Reflect on this.

∽

If you live on this planet, it's not
possible to escape trauma.

Yes, you could summon your trauma
until your last breath,
grabbing on for dear life and not letting go.

Or, you could start with a very different notion:
That every suffering being
in your proximity could benefit
from a kind deed, action, or prayer.

Say a blessing for your own
frail nakedness clothed in eternity.

What more (or less) could one possibly hope for?

Awaken on this!

∽

The Universe is an origami,
and you are a master enfolder of awakening.

If humans possess potential for awakening,
then this potential can only exist because we are
the natural by-product of an awakened
planet and Cosmos.

Is that so hard to believe?

That essence of awakening is already enfolded in
your cells, genes, life and being.

Some call this Buddha Nature,
Christ Consciousness,
Integral Living,
Oneness.

Just as babies innately know to walk,
the power of Here and Now exists within.

Awaken on this.

~

KEY CHAPTER REFERENCES

1. Hartman, H. (2001) *Metacognition in Learning and Instruction.* New York: Springer.

2. Baird B., Mrazek M.D., Phillips, D.T., Schooler J.W. (2014) Domain-specific enhancement of metacognitive ability following meditation training. *Journal of Experimental Psychology: General.* 2014 Oct; 143(5):1972-1979.

3. Coppieters, Frank., (2019) *Unity in Everything That Is.* Conscious Living Media.

4. Newton, J. *Amazing Grace.* https://en.wikipedia.org/wiki/Amazing_Grace (accessed November 2019).

5. Krishnamurti, J. (2009) *Freedom from the Known.* San Francisco: HarperSanfrancisco.

6. Coppieters, F. (2006) *Handbook for the Evolving Heart.* Marina Del Rey, CA: Conflux Press.

7. Zhang, T., Kim, T., Brooks, A.W., et. al. (2014) A "present" for the future: the unexpected value of rediscovery. *Psychological Science.* 2014 Oct. 25(10):1851-60.

8. Norris, G. (2002) *Being Home: Discovering the Spiritual in the Everyday.* Hidden Spring Press.

9. Lao Tzu Quotes, *Goodreads.* https://www.goodreads.com/quotes/2926-be-content-with-what-you-have-rejoice-in-the-way (accessed November 2019).

10. Holt-Lunstad J, Smith TB, Layton JB. Social Relationships and Mortality Risk: A Meta-analytic Review. *PLoS Medicine,* 2010; 7 (7).

11. Emma K. Adam, Louise C. Hawkley, Brigette M. Kudielka and John T. Cacioppo, Day-to-day dynamics of experience-cortisol associations in a population-based sample of older adults. PNAS November 7, 2006 103 (45) 17058-17063.

7

RE-MINDFULNESS FOR STAYING
BALANCED

*C*ongratulations are in order. You have just about reached the end of this course. But before we discuss what you have learned and how to continue to integrate this information into your life to benefit yourself and others, a word of caution needs to be issued about the challenges that face anyone seeking mindfulness. For that reason, let's examine the mountain of choices the average person faces, and how harnessing self-control is critical to a mindfulness practice.

Every person today faces more choices each and every waking 24-hour period than our ancestors faced in a week, a month, or possibly a year. Recent studies (see below) which point out how an overabundance of choice may be affecting us at the brain level by depleting our willpower to resist saying "no" to impulsivity are both surprising and concerning. First, though, let's get a sense of how many choices actually confront us on a daily basis.

Even if we look at something as simple as food choices, the average person makes "well over 200 decisions about food every day," according to food psychologist Brian Wansink.[1] Food-related decisions are not easy to make because they require choosing from an astounding number of items and food combinations. The average supermarket, for instance, features 40,000 different products to choose from, up from close to 10,000 options in 1976 (10,000 seems daunting enough!). The Starbucks coffee shop chain boasts that each customer can now choose from 19,000 different beverage options whenever they enter any store. How about a grande non-fat milk triple-shot hazelnut mocha with whipped cream, cinnamon sprinkles, and a chocolate covered Biscotti to stir it with?

What is more, food is only part of a more complicated decision-making process. In his book *The Paradox of Choice: Why More Is Less*, Barry Schwartz writes, "Comparison shopping to get the best price adds still another dimension to the array choices, so that if you were a truly careful shopper, you could spend the better part of a day just to select a box of crackers, as you worried about price, flavor, freshness, fat, sodium, and calories."[2]

Our ever-expanding palette of choices extends from streaming networks with almost unlimited programming to an endless array of consumer goods, and the trend shows no indication of slowing down. That doesn't include the daily barrage of thousands of advertising-related messages—from billboards to Internet pop-up ads, etc.—that try to grab our attention. Are we really any better off as individuals and as a people because we are exposed to so many choices every day? While there's a real benefit to having so much available at moment's whim, it worth inquiring: How does this exposure erode simplicity and even feelings of self-worth? How can we find the right balance?

EXPERIENCE: REFLECTION ON CHOICE

Reflect upon and answer the following questions:

- *How does an overabundance of choice create feelings of*

being overwhelmed for you?

- *Where in your body or mind do you notice the craving and desire for items? How does constant exposure to these affect those feelings?*

- *Does being overwhelmed by choice trigger you to an unhelpful behavior, such as acting compulsively, numbing yourself out or shutting down?*

WHAT'S NEXT:

Mindfulness of the outer and inner environments is probably the best way to buffer from extremes of choice and impulsivity. These choices and the cravings they produce also offer you more opportunities for practicing presence.

MINDFULNESS FOR SELF-CONTROL AND SELF-REGULATION

A study in the *Journal of Personality and Social Psychology,* after noting that "consumer behavior scientists long have observed that consumers feel frustrated and overwhelmed with the intense information demands that accompany large assortments," went on to describe a series of investigations that the authors conducted which found that too many choices erode our self-control and the ability to self-regulate.[3] Self-regulation was defined by the six study authors as a self-exerting control to override responses in which we replace one response with another to attain a goal.

Using the findings of previous studies, they speculated that self-regulation and decision-making, both aspects of the executive function of the self, draw upon the same resource. You might think of this as being similar to having the strength or energy necessary to move or lift an object.

These researchers were curious whether the proliferation of choices that we in the U.S. must navigate each day might fatigue or deplete this resource (or strength) and result in an overall impairment of self-control. Could having to make so many decisions on a daily basis actually cause someone to lose their willpower and be more susceptible to impulsive or risky behavior?

In four laboratory studies and one field study, groups of undergraduate college students were put through tests in which they made choices from among a variety of consumer goods or college course options. These experiments showed that *making choices led to a reduction in self-control*, which was defined as less physical stamina, reduced persistence in the face of failure, more procrastination, and a diminishment in their arithmetic calculation ability. It also resulted in greater passivity.

"Further studies suggested that choosing is more depleting than merely deliberating and forming preferences about options and more depleting than implementing choices made by someone else," observed the authors, who came from Texas A&M, Florida State, San Diego State, and the University of Minnesota. "The present findings suggest that self-regulation, active initiative, and effortful choosing draw on the same psychological resource. Making decisions depletes that resource, thereby weakening the subsequent capacity for self-control and active initiative."[4]

What also stands out from these findings is that mental fatigue from having to choose from many options can happen quickly. The depletion of the self-regulatory resources through manipulation was frequently induced in as little as 10 minutes.

One of the experiments found this depletion occurred *after just four minutes!*

MINDFULNESS AS SKILLFULNESS

For us to be skillful and functional as human beings, especially in this hectic over-stimulated culture, we must be able to exercise self-control and efficient decision-making. To have that capacity increasingly impaired by the mental fatigue caused by a multiplicity of confusing options and choices, renders us ever more mindless and vulnerable to external manipulation.

Mindfulness skills provide us with enhanced self-control, a natural protective mechanism that replenishes our self-regulatory resource. It offers us this opportunity at a time when we are being overwhelmed by choices and the drumbeat of demands that we 'stimulate the economy' by making even more consumer decisions.

Once you initiate your practice, you can expect to experience some of the benefits rather quickly. There have been studies showing that novices who undertake mindfulness meditation less than 30 minutes a day can improve their moods within a few weeks as if they had taken antidepressants. A 2004 study of 69 breast and prostate cancer patients enrolled in an eight-week Mindfulness-Based Stress Reduction program found "significant improvements" in their stress, sleep quality and overall quality of life no matter how many minutes of home practice or degree of program attendance they undertook.[5]

A 2007 study of a simple mantra-based meditation technique on healthy adults found "that even brief instruction in a simple meditation technique can improve negative mood and perceived stress in healthy adults, which could yield long-term health benefits."[6] A seven-week study of weekly group meditation and its effects on male and female cancer patients with a variety of diagnoses, ages and stages of illness also found these short practices uniformly decreased mood disturbances and stress symptoms.[7]

Other even more significant mindfulness benefits accumulate over time with continued practice. Much research has accumulated showing how mindfulness practices can initiate long lasting changes in brain activity. Added to this work is the 2005 finding from an experiment conducted at Massachusetts General Hospital that long-term meditation actually thickens brain regions associated with attention and sensory processing. Even in older practitioners, their prefrontal cortical thickness was measurably more pronounced "suggesting that meditation might offset age-related cortical thinning," the 13 researchers involved in this study concluded. Meditators evidencing these brain structure changes had meditated an average of once a day for 40 minutes and had from seven to nine years of meditation experience.[8]

Positive changes can occur from mindfulness practices in both the short-term and the long-term. But to initiate a mindfulness practice and then maintain it in this complex consumer culture with so many distractions requires a heightened level of commitment and dedication.

EXPERIENCE: REFLECTION ON SELF-CONTROL

Reflect upon and answer the following questions:

- *In which areas of your life would you like to exert more self-control or limit your choices?*

- *What times in your life have you exercised self-control that felt empowering?*

- *How can mindfulness act as an early warning system to help you recognize thoughts, emotions, or behavior that leads to a loss of self-control or self-regulation?*

WHAT'S NEXT:

Remember, that this is about finding moderation. One needn't live a life of a renunciate to embrace simplicity and peace. If anything, this is about exercising your intention and values as you see fit. You might consider writing down a values statement related to friends, family, career, parenting, and so on. Having these clearly in mind can help you stay inspired to maintain mindfulness.

SIX TIPS FOR A SUCCESSFUL MINDFULNESS PRACTICE

To replace bad habits with better coping skills, a mindfulness practice can be learned within a relatively short period of time. But to actually rewire your brain requires the repetition of that practice over an extended period. That maintenance of practice is an area where everyone needs some support mechanisms in place, especially when 'relapses' to mindless behaviors occur, as they invariably do.

"What happens when we begin to practice mindfulness with some dedication?" asks Michael O'Neal, co-director of the Center for Mindful Living in Minneapolis. "At first—maybe not much. One thing beginning practitioners of mindfulness meditation soon notice is the unbelievable busyness of their minds, and the mind's tenacity in keeping attention focused on its 'stuff.' This can be an uncomfortable discovery. But when we continue to practice mindfulness, with a gentle but firm intention to engage again and again with the way things are right now, we find that the mind *can* quiet down."[9]

Awareness and mindfulness take time to cultivate, so whatever you do, don't give up. With mindfulness, persistence really does pay off. Remember that a relapse is not a failure. Just think of it as an opportunity to develop a new and better plan. Here are some tips for success.

1) **Stay Informed**. One way to keep yourself motivated is to stay informed about the many physical and mental benefits of a mindfulness practice. In this guide you have learned about how it elevates immune system function, decreases blood pressure, improves sleep and digestion, elevates moods and memory, and a host of other benefits. Write out all of these benefits on paper, if necessary, and read the list when you don't feel motivated to practice. Add to that list as new science studies uncover new benefits. Keep yourself constantly aware of why you need to practice.

2) **Start Modestly.** Small steps can lead to big steps. Try mindfulness on for size in a variety of ways at first. See what works best for you. At first, try sitting for three minutes a day in mindfulness meditation, and then add a few minutes each week. Experiment with the many daily mindfulness practices described in this guide. Integrate some of them slowly into your routine. By starting modestly on the mindfulness path, unless you are just naturally a big self-starter, you stand a better chance of maintaining the curiosity and enthusiasm necessary to keep your momentum going.

3) **Stay Regular**. Make your mindfulness practice one of those 'good' habits. Once you find the types of practices and times that work best for you, make a schedule and stick to the schedule. One way to remind yourself is by posting reminder notes. Place the notes, maybe just with the words 'Be Mindful,' in conspicuous places—on a bathroom mirror, a refrigerator door, even on the steering wheel of your vehicle. Keep yourself

aware of your commitment and your conscience will assist in keeping you motivated.

4) Do Journaling. Chart your practice and your progress with it. Do it daily or weekly. Give yourself permission to be open and vulnerable. When you feel resistance to the practice, when you feel lethargy or indifference, write about it in detail. Express yourself but do so with a compassion for your process. Go back and read earlier journal posts periodically to stay aware that your practice is evolving and so are you.

5) Vary Routines. To keep yourself curious and the practice fresh, experiment with varying your routine over time. If you meditate inside of a closet, move it to a corner of a room and meditate behind a screen. If you usually take mindful walks, instead try sitting mindfully as the sun rises or sets. Alternate your techniques periodically, even add new rituals and new elements to old rituals, to stay stimulated.

6) Seek Support. Have you sometimes noticed how much easier it is to exercise if you do it with someone else, or workout with a group at a gym, or have a fitness instructor motivating you? The same may hold true for your mindfulness practice. If you are feeling stuck and unmotivated, find someone or a group to practice with. If you think it necessary, recruit a mindfulness coach, a meditation teacher, or an experienced mentor to encourage you to stay on track. Consciously try to cultivate relationships with other mindful people so you are constantly surrounded by people committed to walking similar paths.

EXPERIENCE: RETURNING TO THE PRESENT MOMENT

Follow along with the instructions below, then start with PART 1.

Fantasies can take many forms, such as the fantasy of owning a new expensive car, winning the lottery, or acquiring vast wealth and material possessions. When you think about it, the object of a fantasy—whether real or imagined—can easily generate numerous desires and feelings. Mental time travel that negatively affects moods is yet another type of fantasy.

To put blinders on and get stuck on fantasies means that you lose the time that could be used to experience the now moment.

Part 1: Count Your Fantasies and Time Travel
No one can make fantasies and desires go away overnight. Just noticing them and knowing them can be a good place to start. The first step in beginning to wake up is to notice fantasies and cravings. Think of this as a practice of becoming a *fantasy and time travel catcher*. Begin by counting or noting your fantasies and time travel. You can spend a day or a week doing this. Each day, from the moment you wake up, you can be observant. Don't be alarmed if you find that you frequently are "somewhere else." You are not alone!

Part 2: Return from Time Travel to the Present Moment
Get in the practice of gently coming back to your present moment surroundings when you notice your thoughts have gone to the future or past. You may even notice how particular themes or trains of thought appear over and over.

Part 3: Cultivate Self-Compassion
Whatever your thoughts, find self-kindness and self-compassion for yourself. Remind yourself that you are simply learning more about the nature of the mind—and gaining insight and greater innersight awareness. Have patience as you train the mind—which can be like a wild mustang.

Reflect on these questions after practicing:

- *Are there any common themes or content in the fantasies or* desires? When do they tend to occur—while traveling, at work, at home, at school?

- How often do you go somewhere other than the here and now? Are there triggers that seem to stimulate fantasies or time travel?

- How could a greater awareness of fantasy be useful? How might mind wandering be helpful in a creative way?

WHAT'S NEXT:

When you are noticing your mind-wandering, you are accessing what is referred to as the brain's salience network to master your ability to refocus back to the present. Eventually, you'll start to notice those moments when you lose self-awareness.

In fact, it was over 120 years ago that psychology visionary William James wrote, "...whether the attention come by grace of genius or dint of will, the longer one does attend to a topic the more mastery of it one has. And the faculty of voluntarily bringing back a wandering attention over and over again is the very root of judgment, character, and will. [...] And education which should improve this faculty would be *the* education *par excellence.*"[10]

A MINDFUL EXPLORATION OF TIME SPENT

Did you ever stop to inventory how you actually spend your

time? The purpose of the inventory on the next two pages is to bring some clarity and explore (without judgment) how you allocate your time. If you find overlap between categories (such as exercise and self-care), do the best you can to choose the most accurate category.

For each of the categories below, write down how much time you spend *on average* doing the activities in that category. You can write this time in increments of 15-minutes, 30-minutes, or hours. Naturally, some activities fit into more than one category. Taking a walk, for example, can fit into both the nature and exercise categories. When you find activities that apply to more than one category, mark your time in both categories.

After you've estimated the time spent in these areas, you can answer the questions that follow.

Self-Care: Pleasant activity, hobby, or relaxation

- Daily Average Time Spent:

Face-to-Face without Interruption: Partner, friends & family

- Daily Average Time Spent:

Technology When Not at Work: TV, electronic devices, social media, DVDs, Internet, texting, e-mail, etc.

- Daily Average Time Spent:

Exercise: Movement, play, chores, and other physical activity

- Daily Average Time Spent:

Appetite: Food, cooking, meals, shopping

- Daily Average Time Spent:

Travel and Scheduling: Planning, organizing, transitioning

- Daily Average Time Spent:

Reflection and Contemplation: Exploration, thought, personal growth

- Daily Average Time Spent:

Nature: Sky gazing, appreciating nature, hiking, playing, etc.

- Daily Average Time Spent:

Work, School and Study

- Daily Average Time Spent:

Sleep

- Daily Average Time Spent:

EXPERIENCE: REFLECTION ON TIME SPENT

Reflect upon and answer the following important questions:

- *How do you feel about the distribution of time spent as it is now? What surprises you most?*

- *What are the challenges that this distribution presents you with?*

- *How could you begin to redistribute your time in ways that would be more fulfilling and in line with your deeper values?*

WHAT'S NEXT:

Becoming aware of how you spend your time is the first step in making adjustments that suit your real needs. There's no right or wrong amount of time that needs to be spent on any of these items. Rather, it's about knowing what is most important to you and setting the kind of healthy boundaries that help you reach your goals.

SUMMING UP

My experience with mindfulness is that we are constantly learning more. Certain things may suddenly make sense and "click" for you. New insights might seem to appear out of the blue. This is an affirmation that the process is working.

In addition, take time to review the *Index of Experiences and Exercises* found on page 171. Refer to this Index as a quick way to locate exercises that you'd like to use again. You might even use this Index to assemble a personalized mindfulness practice. Simply group together those exercises that best fit your needs. However you choose to do this, have fun as you adapt it and make it your own.

For the last exercise in *Simply Mindful*, take this opportunity to review what you have learned about mindfulness. Look back on the many reflections and practices you've completed. Then, reflect on how you will use this knowledge in your daily life, at work and with others.

EXPERIENCE: LOOKING BACK. WHAT DID I LEARN?

Reflect and evaluate what you now know about mindfulness compared to when you began:

- *What is my greatest insight about mindfulness and its practice applications?*

- *What do I think my mindfulness practice will look like three months from now? Six months from now? A year from now?*

- *How do I hope to use mindfulness in my own life and relationships?*

- *How do I hope to use mindfulness in my work or with others?*

- *What will be my biggest obstacle or challenge to maintaining a mindfulness practice?*

- *How will I know that my mindfulness is being effective?*

- *How can I continue to inspire myself and others along the path of presence?*

WHAT'S NEXT:

Your own wisdom and answers to the above-mentioned questions will help you to develop a realistic plan for moving forward. Having completed this course, you now have a lot of direct experience about how to regulate your moods and emotions, as well as enhance your emotional, physical and spiritual well-being.

Congratulations on applying the discipline, persistence, energy and effort necessary to complete the *Simply Mindful* journey. With an awareness of what these practices offer, you are now ready to embark on your own voyage of mindfulness discovery.

MOVING FORWARD ON THE MINDFULNESS JOURNEY

It is my hope that the evidence presented for the simple yet profound power of mindfulness has helped you gain an understanding of how its wider application can improve all human relationships.

These scientifically tested and proven interventions are an exciting antidote to the powerlessness and hopelessness that so many people in our world feel. In the days ahead, make a new habit of applying these practices to real life situations to benefit yourself and others. In this way, may you find many blessings as you experience and spread the calming ripples of mindfulness into the world.

$\sim$

Key Chapter References

1. Wansink, B. (2007) *Mindless Eating: Why We Eat More Than We Think.* New York: Bantam.

2. Schwartz, B. (2005) *The Paradox of Choice: Why More Is Less.* New York: Harper Perennial.

3. Vohs, K.D., et al. (2008) Making Choices Impairs Subsequent Self-Control: A Limited-Resource Account of Decision Making, Self-Regulation, and Active Initiative. *Journal of Personality and Social Psychology.* 2008; 94(5):883-898.

4. same as 3.

5. Carlson, L.E., et al. (2004) Mindfulness-based stress reduction in relation to quality of life, mood, symptoms of stress and levels of cortisol, dehydroeplandrosterone sulfate (DHEAS) and melatonin in breast and cancer outpatients. *Psychoneurodendocrinology.* 2004 May; 29(4):448-474.

6. Lane, J.D., et al. (2007) Brief Meditation Training Can Improve Perceived Stress And Negative Mood. *Alternative Therapies in Health and Medicine.* 2007 Jan/Feb; 13(1):38-50.

7. Speca, M. et al. (2000) A Randomized, Wait-List Controlled Clinical Trial: The Effect of a Mindfulness Meditation-Based Stress Reduction Program on Mood and Symptoms of Stress in Cancer Outpatients. *Psychosomatic Medicine.* 2000; 62:613-622.

8. Lazar, S.W., et al. (2005) Meditation experience is associated with increased cortical thickness. *Neuroreport.* 2005 Nov 28; 16(17):1893-1897.

9. O'Neal, M. (2010) Developing a mindfulness practice. The Center for Mindful Living. Minneapolis, MN: www.oceandharma.org.

10. *PsyBlog*, Jeremy Dean. William James on Attention and the Road to Mastery, https://www.spring.org.uk/2014/02/william-james-on-attention-and-the-road-to-mastery.php (accessed December 2019).

INDEX OF EXPERIENCES AND EXERCISES

∾

FOR FURTHER READING

Altman, Donald, *Reflect: Awaken to the Wisdom of the Here and Now.* Eau Claire, WI: PESI Publishing & Media, 2019
Altman, Donald, *The Mindfulness Toolbox for Relationships.* Eau Claire, WI: PESI Publishing & Media, 2018
Altman, Donald, *101 Mindful Ways to Build Resilience.* Eau Claire, WI: PESI Publishing & Media, 2016
Altman, Donald, *Clearing Emotional Clutter.* Novato, CA: New World Library, 2016
Altman, Donald, *Stay Mindful & Color.* Eau Claire, WI: PESI Publishing & Media, 2016
Altman, Donald, *The Mindfulness Toolbox.* Eau Claire, WI: PESI Publishing & Media, 2014
Altman, Donald, *One Minute Mindfulness.* Novato, CA: New World Library, 2011
Altman, Donald, *The Mindfulness Code: Keys to Overcoming Stress, Anxiety, Fear and Unhappiness.* Novato, CA: New World Library, 2010
Altman, Donald, *Living Kindness.* Portland, OR: Moon Lake Media, 2009
Altman, Donald, *Meal By Meal: 365 Daily Meditations for*

Finding Balance with Mindful Eating. Novato, CA: New World Library, 2004

Altman, Donald, *Art of the Inner Meal.* HarperSanFrancisco, 2000 (hardcover); Portland, OR: Moon Lake Media, 2002 (paperback)

Arden, John, *Mind-Brain-Gene.* New York: W.W. Norton, 2019

Arden, John, *Rewire Your Brain.* New York: Wiley, 2010

Badenoch, Bonnie, *Being a Brain-Wise Therapist: A Practical Guide to Interpersonal Neurobiology.* New York: Norton, 2008

Baer, Ruth, *Mindfulness-Based Treatment Approaches.* Elsevier, Academic Press, University of Kentucky, 2006

Baldoni, John, *Grace: A Leader's Guide to a Better Us.* Pensacola, FL: Indigo River Publishing, 2019

Baldoni, John, *Lead Your Boss: The Subtle Art of Managing Up.* New York: AMACOM, 2009

Begley, Sharon, *Train Your Brain, Change Your Mind.* New York: Ballantine Books, 2007

Benson, H., *The Relaxation Revolution.* New York: Scribner, 2011

Benson, H., *The Relaxation Response.* New York: Harper Collins ebooks, 2009

Brantley, Jeffrey, *Calming Your Anxious Mind.* Oakland, CA: New Harbinger Publications, 2007

Chödrön, Pema, *Start Where You Are: A Guide to Compassionate Living.* Boston: Shambhala, 2001

Coppieters, Frank, *Unity in Everything That Is.* Conscious Living Media, 2019

Coppieters, Frank, *Handbook for the Evolving Heart.* Marina Del Rey, CA: Conflux Press, 2006

Cousins, Norman, *Anatomy of an Illness.* New York: Norton, 1997

Daiensai, Richard Kirsten, *Smile: 365 Happy Meditations,* London: MQ Publications, Ltd., 2004

Diener, Ed; Biswas-Diener, Robert, *Happiness: Unlocking the Mysteries of Psychological Wealth*. Malden, MA: Blackwell Publishing, 2008

Flores, Philip, *Addiction as an Attachment Disorder*. Lanham, MD: Aronson, 2003

Gershon, Michael, *The Second Brain*. New York: Harper, 1999

Gordon, M.D., James, *Unstuck: Your Guide to the Seven-Stage Journey Out of Depression*. New York: Penguin Press, 2008

Hayes, Steven; Follette, Victoria; Linehan, Marsha; editors, *Mindfulness and Acceptance: Expanding the Cognitive Behavioral Tradition*. New York: Guilford Press, 2004

Hüther, Gerald, *The Compassionate Brain: How Empathy Creates Intelligence*. Boston: Trumpeter Books, 2006

Iacoboni, Marco. *Mirroring People: The Science of Empathy and How We Connect with Others*. New York: Picador, 2009

Kabatt-Zinn, Jon; Teasedale, John; Williams, Mark; Zindel Segal; *The Mindful Way Through Depression*. New York: Guilford Press, 2007

Kabatt-Zinn, Jon, *Full Catastrophe Living: Using the Wisdom of Your Body and Mind to Face Stress, Pain and Illness*. New York: Delacorte Press, 1990

Kabatt-Zinn, Jon, *Wherever You Go There You Are: Mindfulness Meditation in Everyday Life*. New York: Hyperion, 1997

Kashdan, Todd, *Curious?: Discover the Missing Ingredient to a Fulfilling Life*. New York: William Morrow, 2009

Kornfield, Jack, *The Art of Forgiveness, Loving-Kindness, and Peace*. New York: Bantam, 2002

Langer, Ellen, *Mindfulness*. Cambridge, MA: Da Capo Press, 2014

Levine, Peter, with Frederick, Ann, *Waking the Tiger: Healing Trauma*. Berkeley, CA: North Atlantic Books, 1997

Lyubomirsky, Sonja, *The How of Happiness*. New York: Penguin, 2008

Marlatt, G. Alan; Bowen, Sarah; Chawla, Neha, *Mindfulness-Based Relapse Prevention for Addictive Behaviors: A Clinician's Guide*. New York: Guilford Press, 2010

McQuaid and Carmona. *Peaceful Mind: Using Mindfulness & Cognitive Behavioral Psychology to Overcome Depression*. Oakland, CA: New Harbinger Publications, 2004

Najavits, Lisa, *Seeking Safety*. New York: Guilford Press, 2001

O'Connor, Richard, *Undoing Perpetual Stress*. New York: The Berkley Publishing Group, 2006

Rosenberg, Larry. *Breath by Breath: The Liberating Practice of Insight Meditation*. Boston: Shambhala, 2004

Salzberg, S., *Loving-Kindness: The Revolutionary Art of Forgiveness*. Boston: Shambhala, 1997

Sapolsky, Robert, *Why Zebras Don't Get Ulcers*. New York: W.H. Freeman and Co., 1994

Segal, Zindel; Williams, Mark; Teasdale, John, *Mindfulness-Based Cognitive Therapy for Depression*. New York: Guilford Press, 2002

Siegel, R.D. *The Mindfulness Solution: Everyday Practices for Everyday Problems*. New York: The Guilford Press, 2010

Schwartz, Barry, *The Paradox of Choice: Why More Is Less*. New York: Harper Perennial, 2005

Schwartz, Jeffrey, *Brain Lock*. New York: Harper Perennial, 2016

Schwartz, Jeffrey, *The Mind & The Brain: Neuroplasticity and the Power of Mental Force*. New York: Harper Perennial, 2003

Shapiro, Shauna, and Carlson, Linda, *The Art and Science of Mindfulness: Integrating Mindfulness into Psychology and the Helping Professions*. Washington, DC: American Psychological Press, 2009

Silananda, U, *The Four Foundations of Mindfulness*. Somerville, MA: Wisdom Publications, 2003

Snyder, C.R., *The Psychology of Hope*. New York: Free Press, 2003

Snyder, C.R. *Handbook of Hope: Theory, Measures and Applications.* 2000. New York: Academic Press.

Snyder, C.R., McDermott, Cook, and Rapoff, *Hope for the Journey: Helping Children Through Good Times and Bad.* New York: Basic Books, 1997

Thich Nhat Hanh, *The Miracle of Mindfulness.* Boston: Beacon Press, 1976

Wansink, Brian, *Mindless Eating: Why We Eat More Than We Think.* New York: Bantam, 2007

Whybrow, Peter, *American Mania: When More Is Not Enough.* New York: Norton, 2006

ONLINE RESOURCES

Donald Altman:
 www.mindfulpractices.com
 facebook.com/mndfulpractices

Awakened Heart Project for Contemplative Judaism:
 www.awakenedheartproject.org

Boundless Way Zen:
 www.boundlesswayzen.org

Cambridge Insight Meditation Center (Vipassanā meditation):
 www.cimc.info

Center for Mindfulness in Medicine, Healthcare, and Society:
 www.umassmed.edu/content.aspx?id=

Center for Mindfulness and Psychotherapy:
 www.mindfulnessandpsychotherapy.org

Contemplative Outreach (contemplative or centering prayer)

www.contemplativeoutreach.org

Dana Foundation (Brain and Immunology):
www.dana.org

Dzogchen Foundation (Tibetan Buddhist tradition):
www.dzogchen.org

Insight Meditation Society (Vipassanā meditation):
www.dharma.org

Laboratory for Affective Neuroscience:
http://psyphz.psych.wisc.edu/

Mindfulnessatwork.org

Social Cognitive Neuroscience Lab, UCLA:
www.scn.ucla.edu

The Center for Mindful Eating:
www.TCME.ORG